50 plus one

Tips to Building a Retirement Nest Egg

by
Linda M. Magoon
&
Poonum Vasishth

Encouragement Press

Information to Encourage Achievement

1261 West Glenlake
Chicago, IL 60660
www.encouragementpress.com

ISBN: 1-933766-02-6
EAN: 978-1-933766-02-7

This product is not intended to provide legal or financial advice or substitute for the advice of an attorney or advisor.

10 9 8 7 6 5 4 3 2 1

©2007 Encouragement Press, LLC
1261 West Glenlake
Chicago, IL 60660

Special discounts on bulk quantities of Encouragement Press books and products are available to corporations, professional associations and other organizations. For details, contact our Special Sales Department at 1.253.303.0033.

50 plus one

Tips to Building a Retirement Nest Egg

About the Authors

Linda M. Magoon has been a retirement planning specialist and human resource manager for nearly 25 years. Her experience includes both for-profit and non-profit organizations. She has been advising employees and managers on medical and retirement benefits, including both qualified and non-qualified plans, through company-sponsored training programs and seminars.

She has a Masters Degree in Educational and Business Management and currently works for a suburban Chicago school system. In addition to her full-time work, she is teaching business classes on the graduate school level. She is the co-author of *50 plus one Tips When Hiring and Firing Employees* (Encouragement, 2007)

Poonum Vasishth has more than 21 years experience in financial consulting. In addition to graduating from Pacific Lutheran University with a B.A. in Business Administration with a finance concentration, she is a Registered Investment Advisor, holds A NASD licensed securities broker license and is also a licensed life and health insurance broker. Poonum's versatility and experience encompasses all aspects of financial planning from working with individuals to develop estate and retirement plans to consulting for small businesses to set-up pension and deferred compensation plans, buy-sell agreements and key-man insurance.

Table of Contents

Buyers of this book are entitled to use free of charge the forms and checklists which are described or illustrated in this book. For your convenience, all forms are available in either Word or Excel on *www.encouragementpress.com.* Click on the tab marked forms and download those forms you require.

Introduction

Retirement is not dull, dreary and depressing…or at least it does not have to be. People retiring today have a huge number of options in terms of life style, personal pursuits and career choices (even full-time, in a different field perhaps). What allows some people to retire early, have the financial well-being to travel, relocate, help their children and generally enjoy life? They planned for retirement while others simply spent and spent, not giving a thought to downsizing or the cost of living well (as opposed to barely making it)!

The truth is out and it is a harsh reality. The vast majority of people do not have a financial plan for retirement or in many cases, do not have a clue on how to start one. Few realize that it will take from 60 percent to 80 percent of their current income to have the same standard of living, the same lifestyle and the same housing they now enjoy. Traditional pension plans are few and far between and Social Security was never intended to pay all the bills (not to mention recreation or travel).

This does not have to be a crisis, but retirement is a very real challenge that we can no longer avoid. Planning and preparation are a must. Retirement planning is nothing more than good, effective financial planning–including learning to manage debt (in fact, reduce it completely), finding ways to save by paying yourself first, understanding more about future Social Security and other retirement benefits to which you may be entitled and more.

50 plus one Tips to Building a Retirement Nest Egg is designed to make your retirement and financial planning easier and safer. Each chapter is devoted to a particular aspect of your financial and business life. Learn:

- How to get out of debt.
- How to save more and sooner.
- How to use credit cards and mortgage debt wisely.
- How a SEP account can assist small business owners.

- How reverse mortgages work.
- How to retire early, or even if you should.

Be wise in the ways of money. Take retirement and your financial well-being seriously. Be active in the process. It is not all that difficult and it is something that each of us can and should start immediately. We have developed a number of worksheets available on the Encouragement Press Website, *www.encouragementpress.com*, to help you get started.

The best advice ever given was to the question–When should I start planning for retirement? The answer, of course, is the first day of work. The earlier you start, the more you will have in retirement and the easier and cheaper it will be.

While there are financial pundits all over the place who will sell you retirement advice, none of them will give you as much, as efficiently, as we have in this book. Start today and plan for the future. You will be happy you did.

Linda M. Magoon
Poonum Vasishth

plus one

Everyone Needs a
Retirement Plan

The Challenge

Who needs a retirement plan? Everyone needs a retirement plan! Regardless of your age and when you plan to retire you need a plan. For many people, creating a retirement plan is not the difficult part rather sticking to it is the challenge. It is easy to think up excuses or reasons why today is not the day to start your planning especially if your retirement may be decades away. If you are just beginning your working career the idea of planning for retirement, 30, 40 or even 50 years from now may seem like a very long way away.

The Social Security Administration has issued this warning to all future retirees who have not reached age 55—Unless changes are made, at age 71 in 2041, scheduled benefits could be reduced by 26 percent and could continue to be reduced every year thereafter from presently scheduled levels. This prediction applies to anyone who is in their 20s or older. The message? Start planning now or risk not having enough money put away to retire.

So at the risk of sounding redundant, everyone needs a retirement plan. Whether you are just starting out or nearing retirement, it is never too late to start a savings plan. In this chapter we will discuss the importance of saving for your golden years and how you can create and stick to a savings program you can live with. Your challenge is to develop a retirement plan based on your investment comfort level and start saving!

The Facts

According to a recent government survey:

- Two in five workers say they are not too willing (19 percent) or not at all willing (15 percent) to cut back on their spending in order to save for retirement.

- Almost 7 in 10 workers (68 percent) expect to work into retirement but 4 in 10 retirees end up having to leave the workforce earlier than expected due to health problems, disability or company downsizing.
- Despite estimates by financial experts that retirees will need 70 to 80 percent of their current income to meet everyday living expenses, nearly 40 percent of all workers dismiss this expert advice and think they will need less then 70 percent of their pre-retirement income to live comfortably after leaving the workforce.
- Almost two-thirds (64 percent) of workers do not expect their standard of living to decline in retirement.
- Four out of 10 people aged 55 or older have saved less than $100,000 toward their retirement.
- One out of four workers do not sign up for their employer's 401(k) retirement savings plan and only one in 10 contributes the maximum amount allowed.
- Nearly one-half of all American workers do not contribute enough to their company's 401(k) savings plan to get the full company matching funds.
- Only 19 percent of workers were able to correctly state when they would be eligible for Social Security benefits (the current retirement age is 67 years).

These statistics show that fewer than 25 percent of workers are thinking ahead to their retirement. It is never too late to start saving. Set an investment goal and begin funding it. If you are unsure how much money you will need at retirement there are several good retirement calculators you can use to figure out how much money you will need when you retire and how much you will need to put away before you retire. Online retirement calculators are available at *www.aarp.org*, *www.ssa.gov* and *www.socialsecurity.org*. Knowing your goal will determine how much money you put away today.

If you do not know how you are spending your money today it will be difficult to plan for tomorrow. Here are few ideas to help you begin:

Get a rough idea of your future retirement income by considering both your current retirement investments and the amount you are saving annually. Review the spreadsheet located at the end of Chapter 6: *What You Must Save* to find your proposed retirement age and current income. This will show you how much you have to save.

Calculate your current net worth, which is the total value of everything you own, minus any debts you have to repay and your budget (or cash flow.) This shows your monthly income and spending patterns and creates a snapshot of how money flows in and out of your life each month. An example of a cash flow worksheet is available as a download at *www.encouragementpress.com*.

Estimate the amount of time you need to fully fund your retirement nest egg. Time is the biggest factor in investing. The relationship between time and amount of money you need to save to meet your goals.

Understand how your retirement age affects retirement resources other than savings. This includes Social Security, pensions, dividends, royalties or annuity payouts. Delaying retirement from age 59½ to 65 will increase your benefits.

Decide what type of an investor you are: cautious, moderate or aggressive. The closer you are to retirement the more conservative you may plan.

The Solution

Start by developing a simple, easy to implement plan to start saving. American Association of Retired Persons (AARP) advises its members to think about:

- In how many years do you plan to retire?
- When does your spouse, if any, plan to retire?
- What do you plan to do during retirement?
- Will it require any investment?
- Where do you plan to live?
- What big-ticket expenses are likely to occur before you retire?
- What kind of insurance do you have now?
- What will you need when you retire?
- How much income will you need to live comfortably?
- Where will it come from?

Here are a few simple and immediate steps you can take today, to jump-start your retirement plan.

Pay off your debts. Figure out how much you could put toward paying off your credit card balances. Allocate fewer dollars to your monthly miscellaneous expenses so you can begin paying more towards your monthly minimum payment on each card to pay them off as quickly as possible. Of course, this only works if you cut up and close the credit card accounts so you do not continue charging on them while paying them off.

Sign up to participate in your employer-sponsored 401(k), 403(b) retirement plan or profit sharing plan. You may participate to have your employer automatically deduct a certain amount of money (determined by you) from your regular paycheck and deposit it directly into your retirement account. The benefits to employer-sponsored retirement plans are:

- Implemented by your company making it easy to participate.
- The deduction is automatic forcing you to save.

- Company match programs help increase your savings.
- Some or all of your contribution will be deducted before taxes so it will help reduce your tax liability.

Make one extra mortgage payment per year or make an extra principal payment each month. This will lower the total amount of principal owed on your mortgage and reduces the amount of interest you will pay over the life of the loan and cut years off your mortgage.

Itemize your total expenses for one month. Record everything including bills paid, miscellaneous expenses by date, etc. At the end of the month categorize your spending to see where you may be able to cut back. Just knowing where your money is going will force you to think before you spend in the future.

Consolidate high interest credit card debt into a lower interest rate loan. If you apply for a lower interest credit card read the fine print carefully. The lower rate may only be a promotional rate that increases after a few months. If the interest rate is very low and you plan to pay off a balance within the low rare period you can save a lot on interest charges.

Review your utility bills each month to check for unexplained spikes such as an increase in water use (you may have a leak) or a change in electric or gas usage. Visit each utility company's Website for suggestions on ways to decrease your bills. If you live in an area with extreme temperature change sign up for the budget plan. The budget plan bills you the same amount each month making it easier for you to budget your money.

Review your insurance policies. Are you paying for more coverage than you need? Can you save money on your premium by increasing your deductible? It is worth a few minutes every 6 months to review coverage amount and compare prices with other insurance companies.

If you find it difficult to save, fill out our Cash Flow Worksheet to determine areas where you can review and make changes. You may be surprised to find extra money you can put towards building your retirement nest egg. The spreadsheet is available for download at *www.encouragementpress.com*. Fill in the blanks to find out how much you start saving to enjoy financial freedom in your retirement.

Next determine what kind of an investor you are. Are you conservative, moderate or aggressive? Complete an investor profile questionnaire to help you create a plan that fits your comfort level. To determine what type of investor you are, fill out the *What Type of Investor am I?* worksheet on the next page.

What Type of Investor am I?

Your Risk Tolerance	Point Value	Your Score
If you received a large amount of money, how would you invest it?		
I would invest in a fund that offered moderate current income and was very conservative.	3 points	
I would invest in a fund that offered high current income with a moderate amount of risk.	6 points	
I would invest in a fund that offered high total return with a moderately high amount of risk.	9 points	
I would invest in a fund that offered substantial capital appreciation even though it has a high amount of risk.	12 points	
Which of the following statements best describes your reaction if the value of your portfolio were to suddenly decline by 15%?		
I would be very concerned because I cannot accept fluctuations in the value of my portfolio.	3 points	
If the amount of income I receive remains unaffected then it would not bother me.	6 points	
I would be concerned about even a temporary decline.	9 points	
I accept temporary fluctuations due to market influences.	12 points	
Which of the following investments would you feel most comfortable owning?		
Certificates of deposit	3 points	
U.S. Government securities	6 points	
Large company stocks	9 points	
Stocks of new growth companies	12 points	
Which of the following investments would you least like to own?		
Stocks of new growth companies	3 points	
Large company stocks	6 points	
U.S. Government securities	9 points	
Certificates of deposit	12 points	
Which of the following investments do you feel are the most ideal for your portfolio?		
Certificates of deposit	3 points	
U.S. Government securities	6 points	
Large company stocks	9 points	
Stocks of new growth companies	12 points	

How optimistic are you about the long-term prospects for the economy?		
Very pessimistic	3 points	
Unsure	6 points	
Somewhat optimistic	9 points	
Very optimistic	12 points	

Which best describes your attitude about investments outside the U.S.?		
Unsure	3 points	
I believe the U.S. economy and foreign markets are interdependent.	6 points	
I believe that overseas markets provide attractive investment opportunities.	9 points	

Your Investment Objectives	**Point Value**	**Your Score**
Which of the following best describes your investment objectives?		
Preserving principal with low volatility.	3 points	
Grow capital with moderate volatility.	6 points	
Generating such current income and growing my assets over an extended time frame.	9 points	
Growing my assets substantially over an extended time frame while accepting high volatility.	12 points	
How do you expect your standard of living five years from now to compare to your standard of living today?		
Less than it is today.	3 points	
The same as it is today.	6 points	
Somewhat higher than it is today.	9 points	
Substantially greater than it is today.	12 points	
Five years from today, you expect your portfolio value to be:		
Portfolio value is not my primary concern; I am more concerned with current income.	3 points	
The same as or slightly more than it is today.	6 points	
Greater than it is today.	9 points	
Substantially greater than it is today.	12 points	
Generating current income from your portfolio is:		
A primary concern (only if you are about to retire).	2 points	
Not important.	4 points	
With the income generated from your portfolio, you plan to:		
Use it for living expenses.	2 points	
Use some and reinvest some.	4 points	
Reinvest all income.	6 points	

Your Time Frame	Point Value	Your Score
What is your investment horizon?		
5-10 years	1 point	
10-20 years	2 points	
20-30 years	3 points	
30+ years	4 points	
What is your primary financial goal?		
Wealth preservation.	1 point	
Retirement planning.	2 points	
Wealth accumulation.	3 points	
When do you plan on drawing income?		
5-10 years	1 point	
10-20 years	2 points	
20+ years	3 points	

Determining your investment profile and recommended portfolio:

When you have answered all of the questions, tally up your individual scores according to each section: Risk Tolerance, Investment Objectives and Time Frame. Put each number in the appropriate box then total them to determine your Investment Profile Score.

Risk Tolerance Score	
Investment Objective Score	
Time Frame Score	
Investment Profile Total	

Scoring ranges are assigned for each model, from most aggressive to most conservative.

Your score indicates the type of investor you are:

Scoring Range	Your Investor Profile
115-125	**Aggressive** Aggressive growth focuses on earning maximum capital appreciation.
100-114	Aggressive with growth (Aggressive/Moderate) Growth focuses on growth of principal with little emphasis on current income.
84-99	Growth with income (**Moderate**) Growth with income focuses primarily on growth of principal with an additional focus on current income.
58-83	Income with moderate growth (**Moderate/Conservative**) Income with moderate growth focuses on income, with growth of principal being an important consideration.
34-57	Income with capital preservation (**Conservative**) Income with capital preservation focuses on income with growth of principal being a secondary concern.

In this chapter we have outlined the importance of planning, how to plan, where you can cut from your current budget to begin a saving plan and the type of investor you are, it is time to create your plan. What are you waiting for? There is no time like the present.

The Resources

Visit these Websites to help you begin your planning.

www.aarp.org

American Association of Retired Persons

www.ssa.gov

Social Security Organization

www.socialsecurity.org

The CATO organization

Pay Yourself First

1

The Challenge

According to statistics, the average person today who participates in a savings program saves only about 4 percent of his or her income. That means that each person works less than 30 minutes a day for himself.

Financial advisors agree that in order to create a retirement strategy you must pay yourself first. This is the strategy many people use to force themselves to save money. The theory is that instead of saving whatever is left at the end of the month, you pay yourself first at the beginning of the month.

Paying yourself first turns around the age-old problem of spending until it is all gone. Most workers, when asked, will admit they live paycheck to paycheck, making it difficult to save for the future. You can turn that around simply by taking 1 percent of your income and putting it into a saving account at the beginning of the month. If you do not see it, you will not spend it. Plus, you will have the satisfaction of knowing that when all the money is gone that you have at least saved a portion of your earnings.

Your challenge, then, is to learn how to save and invest your money today in order to enjoy the benefits from it when you need it most–at retirement.

The Facts

These statistics mentioned in the previous chapter bear repeating just in case they did not sink in the first time:

- The proportion of workers who are saving for retirement has remained unchanged since 2001.
- Almost seven in 10 workers (68 percent) expect to work past retirement age, but four in 10 retirees end up having to leave the work force earlier than expected due to health problems, disability or company downsizing.

- Two in five workers say they are not too willing (19 percent) or not at all willing (15 percent) to cut back on their spending in order to save for retirement.
- Four out of 10 people aged 55 or older have less than $100,000 saved toward their retirement.
- One out of four workers do not sign up for their employer's 401(k) retirement saving plan and only one in 10 contributes the maximum amount allowed.
- Nearly half of all American workers do not contribute enough to their company's 401(k) savings plan to get the full company matching funds.
- About half cash out their 401(k) savings when they change jobs instead of rolling it over into an IRA to avoid tax implications and to continue saving and investing for their retirement.

Are you a spender or a saver? What can you cut out of your daily budget that would enable you to save towards your retirement? You need a plan.

The Solution

The budget is already tight, so how are you supposed to find more money to put away for retirement? By shifting your priorities and your budget so you pay yourself first. Here are some quick and very effective solutions to saving money:

- When you sit down to write your bills, the first check you should write is to yourself. Decide on an amount you will pay yourself each month for the next 6 months then deposit that check into your Roth IRA, mutual fund or annuity account.
- If you participate in a direct deposit program, most companies will allow you to put a portion of your paycheck into your checking and savings account. The deduction is done for you. If you do not participate in a direct deposit program, make it a habit to include a percentage of the check into your savings account when you cash the check.
- This principal also works with your 401(k) fund. You may have a portion of your check deposited into your 401(k) account–pretax. This forced savings plan is popular with many people who know it will be difficult for them to save any other way.
- Start by saving a small portion of your check, maybe one percent. Some financial planners believe you should pay yourself at least 1 hour's worth of income every day or 12.5 percent of your gross income. You can gradually increase the amount to 2 percent of your gross pay or 2 hours a day worth of work. The table on the next page illustrates how much you can save using this method of saving.

Your Gross Annual Income	One hour of salary	Savings during a 10 year period	Savings during a 30 year period
$25,000	$12	$3,727	$19,974
$50,000	$24	$7,454	$39,948
$75,000	$36	$11,180	$59,923
$100,000	$48	$13,354	$71,574.24
$150,000	$72	$22,361	$119,845

(based on a 2,088 hour work year with 24 paychecks and generating a 5 percent interest rate per year).

- Starting a pay yourself program is easiest when you get a raise in pay or bonus. Take the increase and put it into your savings account each payday. You will still have the same amount of money available to pay bills and you will not miss the added income. Do not let the fact you will not receive a pay increase for a few more months deter you from beginning to save now.
- You can also make a goal of how much you want to save by the end of the year and work backwards. For example, if you want to save $10,000 for the year you would divide $10,000 by 26 paychecks (if you are paid every other week or 24 times if you are paid twice a month). To reach the goal you will need to deposit $384 or $416 dollars each paycheck into a savings or retirement fund.

$10,000 divided by 26 paychecks = $384 into a retirement account

It is easy to spend every penny in your checking account each month. It is difficult to discipline yourself to save a portion of your income each month for your future retirement and unexpected expenses.

If you still find your budget too tight to save, track each day's expenses for 1 week. You may be amazed at how you spend your money. Instead of buying lunch at a fast food place or store each day consider bringing your lunch once or twice a week. That could save you $10. Instead of going out to a movie for $20, consider staying in and renting a recently released DVD instead and save $15. There, you just saved $25 in one week. Try to save $50 a month using this method and you will save $600 a year. Not a bad start.

Once you become more comfortable with paying yourself first, you can increase the amount you save. A little discipline today will have you patting yourself on the back when you are 64.

The Resources

www.debtguru.com/debtguru/articles/pay-it-forward.html

The Internet domain for the American Credit Foundation®, an IRS 501(c)(3) non-profit consumer credit counseling organization, for a self-help article on paying yourself first.

www.womens-finace.com/challenge/payyourself.shtml

Articles and information on women's finances and financial advice.

www.tomorrowsmoney.org/section.cfm/389/466

Calculate your future retirement needs. This calculator on this site is designed to help you assess your current financial situation and give you an idea of how to begin saving toward the retirement lifestyle you desire.

2

First Step!
Get Out of Debt

The Challenge

Debt is unavoidable. Carrying debt has its benefits and pitfalls. Taking on debt is not necessarily a bad thing. Debt can be beneficial if you are planning on financing an education, buying a home or paying for emergency medical treatment. The interest paid on a mortgage loan (long-term credit) or an equity line of credit is still tax deductible and is generally lower than other types of consumer loans (short-term credit). Establishing a good credit history will save you money as lenders will offer better loan rates to individuals who have proven they are a lower risk.

But then there is debt that works against you. This type of bad debt is when you spend more than you bring in and must rely on loans or another means of financing to pay for everyday living. Most people spend 10 percent more than they make, which means there are many people who rely on credit cards to bridge the gap. This type of debt is not tax deductible and will reduce the amount of money you can save for retirement.

Here is an eye-opening fact: If you took your credit card payment of $250 a month and put it into a retirement account, in 25 years you will have $131,116 in the bank (based on an average long-term return rate of 5 percent; at an 8 percent return the amount increases to $190,289). This illustrates how debt not only costs you thousands of dollars in interest, but also how it prohibits you from adequately saving for your retirement.

The Facts

- The average household has 10 credit cards.
- The average household has a total credit card balance of approximately $25,800.
- The average credit card debt is $8,500.
- The typical minimum monthly credit card payment is 90 percent interest

and 10 percent principal.

- Sixty-five percent of all credit card accounts have only the minimum payment amounts being made by consumers.
- Almost one-half of all households in America report having difficulty paying their minimum monthly payments.
- Americans paid out approximately $82 billion in interest alone last year.
- A survey by the Consumer Bankers Association found that, within a year, 70 percent of the people who had shifted credit card balances to home equity were again running up credit card debt.
- If your credit card balance is $8,000 and you make the minimum monthly payment at 18 percent interest, it will take you 25 years, 7 months to pay off the debt. You will pay $15,432 in interest charges (almost twice the balance), bringing your total paid to $23,432.
- On average the typical credit card purchase is 112 percent higher than if paying cash.

The Solution

Identifying how you got into debt trouble is easy; creating a plan to get out of it is more difficult. Knowing your credit limit is key to staying out of financial trouble. Suggestions to help you stay out of the black hole:

- Do everything you can to pay off your credit card balances every month. If you use a credit card to gain mileage or reward points, be aware that for every balance you carry the points you accumulate are costing you money. Most credit cards have interest rates between 13.5 percent and 21 percent. Paying that kind of interest, except in extreme cases, is costing you big in the long-term.
- If you must carry a balance each month make larger payments than the required minimum. If your statement shows a $0 minimum amount due but you still have a balance, always make a payment. The minimum payment amount simply covers the interest amount due on the principal and does not pay any portion of the principal. If you only pay the minimum you will never pay off the card. While you are working to pay off the balance stop using the card until the balance is paid off.
- If the minimum payments are becoming too difficult to pay, call your credit card company and ask them to lower the interest rate. If your payment history with the card has been good they will often work with you and offer you a lower rate. It will be difficult to convince a finance company to lower your rate if your payments to them have been spotty or if you have missed several payments in the past.

- Find one of those credit cards with a low introductory rate. Some cards offer 1 percent or 3.9 percent rates on transfer balances. While the interest rate is low, make a determined effort to get it paid off. Put the card away and do not use it until the card is paid off.
- Consolidate your debts by taking out a home-equity loan and pay them off. The interest is tax-deductible and is lower than the credit card interest rate. A key to making this work is to cut up or put away the credit card while you are paying it off via the home-equity loan. Using the card will wipe out any gains you may be making.
- If your plan is to pay off the balance every month, record each credit card purchase into your checkbook as if you had written a check. When the bill comes in, you have already accounted for the payment required in your checkbook and you can write the check without worrying where the cash will come from.
- Use your savings to get out of debt and know that you can always charge an emergency on your credit card. Take the interest charges you are not incurring every month and put that money towards retirement.
- Periodically review your finances from a lender's point of view. Calculate your debt to income ratio yearly or even every 6 months. To calculate your DTI Ratio, divide your debt by your income. If you ratio is above 25 percent, you need to find a way to reduce it. Even if you are not planning on borrowing money, the fact that you are overextended will limit how much you can save towards your retirement.
- Total up your bills. The total amount due each month is all that matters. No matter how well you think your are doing as you go along, allocate the same amount to monthly payments every month.
- Pay off the smallest bills first, leaving more to allocate to the larger ones as you go along. Example: You have two bills due at the same time, one for $250 and one for $750, for a total of $1,000. You can afford to pay $500 a month. Pay off the smaller one, and put the remaining $250 on the larger one. Once the smaller bill is paid off you can pay more towards the next largest bill until that is paid off and so on. This strategy assumes that there is no interest attached to late payments.
- Give yourself reasonable deadlines. Avoid sabotaging your own financial plans. Set reasonable goals you can stick to. If you owe $1,000 divide the payments by 12 months and pay $85 a month.

You have five credit cards with a total balance of almost $20,000 at various rates between 9 percent and 21 percent.

Credit Card	APR	Current Balance	Monthly Payment	Time Needed to Pay Off
Visa	21%	$2,400	$216.33	9 months
MasterCard	21%	$5,000	$100.00	1 year, 5 months
Discover	19%	$4,500	$200.00	1 year, 9 months
Store Card	14%	$3,500	$150.00	2 years
AMEX	9%	$4,500	$300.00	2 years

You can pay these amounts down in many ways. You can pay $966.33 a month and it will take you 2 years to pay off your credit cards. This is the quickest method. Based on your current combined balance of $19,900.00, you will pay a total of $3,303.87 in interest. Your strategy would be to pay as much as your budget allows to the credit card with the highest interest rate, and pay the minimum to your lower rate cards.

If you choose to pay only the minimum amount due, it will take you up to 56 years and 6 months to pay off your credit cards. Based on your current combined balance of $19,900, you will pay a total of $31,373.73 in interest. That is quite a difference.

Use any one of several credit payoff calculators available on the Web to create a payoff plan for all your bills. These debt reduction calculators let you enter in the balances you owe and then show you how long it will take to become debt free and how much you will pay in interest by making the minimum monthly payments.

This is an excellent way to see exactly what you owe, how you can pay it off quickly and start putting this money towards your retirement.

The Resources

http://cgi.money.cnn.com/tools/debtplanner/debtplanner.jsp

CNN/Money magazine offers an excellent debt reduction calculator. Input your card name, balances, interest rate and minimum monthly payments to find out how long it will take you to become debt free.

www.gawwk.com

This Website offers personal debt statistics-information and resources.

www.Top-3-sites.com

Top 3 sites lists the most commonly accessed sites on personal debt.

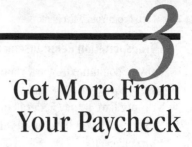

Get More From Your Paycheck

The Challenge

The little things can really add up. Take your paycheck, for example. A few small adjustments, such as changing your withholding designation and taking advantage of pre-tax withholdings, can lead to big dividends down the road.

This chapter suggests several small changes you can try to squeeze more out of your paycheck. The money you gain can be added to your retirement or savings plans without putting the squeeze on your budget.

The Facts

Do you find it difficult to save money? Do you consider your annual tax refund as a forced savings plan? Do you live paycheck to paycheck? Do you keep putting off contributing to your retirement plan? If so, you are in good company. According to a national online survey conducted by the American Payroll Association (APA), more than two-thirds of American workers live paycheck to paycheck and would be cash-strapped if their paycheck was delayed a week.

The Solution

Put the squeeze on your paycheck without putting the squeeze on your budget. Here are a few suggestions for getting more from your paycheck.

Pre-tax automatic withdrawal programs can save you money:

- Transportation Reimbursement Incentive Programs (TRIP)
- 529 College Savings Plans
- Dependent and Child Care Flexible Spending Accounts
- Health Care Flexible-Spending Accounts
- Health Savings Accounts
- 401(k) Saving Account
- Adjust your withholding

Transportation Reimbursement Incentive Programs (TRIP)

If you commute to work via public transportation, you can reduce your transportation costs and your taxes. An automatic TRIP deduction means you do not have to pay Federal and FICA taxes on commuting-related parking or transit expenses if you have money deducted from your paycheck before taxes are calculated.

529 College Savings Plan

A 529 College Savings Plan is an attractive savings program if you or a family member plan to attend college. Money withdrawn is federal tax-free as long as it is applied to qualified education expenses. Any money left over in the account can be transferred to siblings of the same generation without triggering federal gift or federal income taxes.

Dependent Care/Child Care Flexible Spending Accounts

Dependent Care Flexible Spending Accounts help defray the cost of work related to dependent care, child care or day care. Money is deducted pre-tax from your paycheck to be used to cover costs associated with qualified childcare, day care, camps or dependent care. Be aware, however, this is a use it or lose it type of account. If your deductions are higher than your expenses during the year you may lose the unused portion (similar to a health care flexible spending account).

Health Care Flexible Spending Accounts (FSA)

A Flexible Spending Account allows you to contribute pre-tax dollars towards health and dependent care expenses. Participating in an FSA can reduce your federal income taxes, Social Security taxes, Medicare taxes and state and local taxes in most states. These accounts are set up similar to Dependent Care/Child Care Accounts in that money is deducted pre-tax to cover the cost of prescription, dental, health and vision expenses. Money deducted during the year must be spent on medical procedures performed during the year. You cannot roll this money over to the following year. You have only 10 weeks (March 15th) of the following year to apply the money to qualified expenses or risk losing left over money.

Health Savings Accounts (HSA)

Health Savings Accounts are high-deductible health plans, also known as consumer-driven plans, that enable you to pay a lower share of your insurance premiums in exchange for a larger deductible. If your employer offers a health savings account plan, you can contribute to a tax-free account to cover the deductible. Health savings accounts let you roll over unused money from year to year. If you switch employers, you can take the money with you. You can use the money to pay for eligible medical expenses or save it for retirement; as long as withdrawals are used to pay for qualified expenses, you will not pay taxes on them. There is no time limit to using the funds. The only limitation is you can only contribute the amount equal to your deductible. If your deductible is $1,000, that is the maximum you can contribute each year.

401(k) Saving Account

A 401(k) is an employer-sponsored retirement savings plan, funded by the employee through pre-tax payroll deductions. The biggest attraction to this type of plan is money contributed is federal and state tax-deferred until the money is withdrawn. You manage your own account and may have several investment plans to select from. Money is deducted directly from your check, making it easy to save. Contributions may start out small and may be increased with pay raises or bonuses. If you change jobs you can transfer your money to your new employer's plan or a different IRA. Your company may match your contributions to your 401(k) account. Sometimes this matching program can be as high as 50 percent, but typically is up to 6 percent. If you contribute 10 percent of your salary each paycheck to your retirement account and your company is willing to match you contribution up to 6 percent, this is a great way to increase your contribution by 60 percent.

Adjust Your Withholding

Adjust your withholding so your tax payments match your actual tax liability. This is especially important anytime you have a major life change, such as marriage or divorce, the birth or adoption of a child or the purchase of a home. If you do not have enough income taxes taken out, you will owe money to Uncle Sam at the end of the year and you may be assessed a big penalty and interest charges. If you have too much taken out, you are giving the government free use of your money–money that could be making interest for you.

If you receive a $1,000 refund from your taxes each year you are losing more than you think. During a 5-year period, the money that Uncle Sam is holding each year is costing you approximately $700 in lost interest. For example: If you put away $83.33 each month for 1 year for a total of $1,000, you would have $5,666.95 at the end of the fifth year (based on a 5 percent annual compounded rate).

Year	Monthly Deposit	Ending Balance	Balance + 5% Interest
1	$83.33	$ 999.96	$1,023.20
2	$83.33	$1,999.92	$2,098.74
3	$83.33	$2,999.88	$3,229.32
4	$83.33	$3,999.84	$4,417.73
5	$83.33	$4,999.80	$5,666.95

The Resources

www.kiplinger.com/personalfinance/

Kiplinger's Personal Finance monthly magazine.

www.chif.com/a/Budget-Paycheck.htm

Getting the most from your paycheck article.

www.adp.com/mypaycheck/

Maximizing your paycheck article.

www.bankrate.com/brm/itax/tips/20010124a.asp

Tax Tip #22, How to adjust your withholding.

www.irs.gov/individuals/article/0,,id=96196.html

IRS withholding calculator from the Department of Treasury helps you find out the right amount to withhold from your earnings.

www.asbhawai.com/calculators/savings.php

American Savings Bank Deposit/Savings Amortization Calculator.

www.fool.com/calcs/calculators.htm

Access retirement calculators.

How Much to Contribute Each Year?

The Challenge

How much to contribute to your retirement portfolio depends on your age and how much you have already saved. If you are just starting a career or planning your retirement in say…40 or 45 years, saving for retirement is probably not a high priority. When you are in your 20s you are in your acquisition stage. This is the age when you need more immediate items like a couch, car and a career wardrobe, and when you begin to pay for your own insurance, rent, utilities and food. After paying for life expenses and taxes there is little left for investing in something that is almost half a century away. That big span of time is precisely the reason why you should be putting away as much as possible each month now. Even a small amount of saving will reap big benefits over time.

The Facts

Consider this: If starting at age 25 you put away $6,461.54 each year into a retirement fund, you will have amassed $1 million by age 65.

If you are age 50+ and just starting to think about saving for retirement, you still have time to get in the game. However, you will have to part with more money each year to reach the same $1 million. If you start with a base retirement amount of $25,000, you must save $43,933.73 each year until you are age 65 to save $1 million. For 401(k) and similar retirement plans, you can contribute up to $15,000 tax deferred. A similar provision allows workers age 50 or older to contribute up to $18,000.

This illustrates the importance of starting your savings plan earlier rather than later. However, it is never too late to save for retirement. It is only too late if you do not save at all. Whether you are only a few years away from your last day of work or 50 years, every little bit you can save counts.

The Solution

Set Goals and Estimate Your Expenses

First, decide how much money you will need to live in the retirement lifestyle you want. With good health, your retirement could last 30 years or more. The estimated life expectancy of a male today is 82 years old. How much money will you need to pay bills in retirement? What are your goals? Do you want to travel? What is the cost of living where you plan to live? Will your mortgage be paid off?

Once in retirement, you will be spending a greater portion of your retirement savings on medical expenses. What other debts do you need to think about? Your answers to these questions are important as they will help you decide how much money you will need to save for a comfortable retirement. By knowing how much money you can count on and how much you expect to spend, you can decide how much you need to save. Financial experts typically say you will need at least 70 percent of your pre-retirement income to live comfortably in retirement.

To understand where your post-retirement income will come from, make a checklist of all the sources of income you can count on. These may include:

Retirement Income Source	Monthly income
Social Security	$
401(k), 403(b), or 457 accounts	$
Traditional and Roth Individual Retirement Accounts (IRAs)	$
Savings and investments	$
Inheritance (trust fund)	$
Employment	$
Annuity	$
Home equity, rental property or reverse mortgage	$
Miscellaneous other income	$
Total	$

Is the total amount enough for you to live comfortably? If you have been slow to save for retirement and need to play catch-up, there are several ways for you to make up for lost time.

Retirement Plan Options

A good place to start is to contribute more each year to your employer-sponsored retirement plan, such as a 401(k), 403(b) or 457 plan. Put as much money as you are allowed ($15,000) into these tax-deferred accounts. This is especially beneficial if your employer makes matching contributions because this is bonus money that you lose by not participating. The pre-tax contribution limits for these types of plans will increase over the next few years. Traditional IRAs are funded pre-tax, thus reducing your taxable income. You pay taxes on the money when you start withdrawing the money when you retire.

Roth IRAs also provide an opportunity to save for retirement, but are funded with after-tax contributions. This means taxes have already been deducted from the income and you do not receive a current year tax deduction for these contributions. However, all contributions and earnings are income tax free when you withdraw funds once you retire. This holds true as long as you have had the account for at least 5 years and are at least 59½ years old when you begin making withdrawals. For regular and Roth IRAs, the yearly contribution limit is $4,000 in 2006 and increases to $5,000 in 2008.

Finally, many people are self-employed or work for themselves in addition to their regular job. They have several tax-deferred options from which to choose, including SEP-IRA and SIMPLE-IRA plans. Depending on your income you can contribute as much as $40,000 a year into a retirement fund.

Money you save now has the better chance to grow until you are ready to use it. It may be hard to jump from not saving at all to setting aside large amounts of money. But start small and build your savings over time. Here are some helpful tips:

- Decide how much you want to save each month and have it automatically deducted from your paycheck or write yourself a check each month. Do not use it for anything else unless you absolutely have to.
- Make saving for your retirement a top priority. Think of it as a mortgage or utility expense that you have to budge for.
- Do not be too conservative in your investment strategy. Consider investing in diversified stock mutual funds to lower your risks and boost your returns. Balance your portfolio to include high, medium and low risk investments.
- By saving all you can now, you will reap the rewards of compound interest. Compound interest earns you interest on interest. In other words, interest is paid on the original amount you save plus the interest you earn along the way.
- Look into the equity you have built in your home. You could move to a less expensive area if you want to downsize during retirement. If you sell your home, you may be able to pay off your mortgage–maybe even invest a significant portion of the monies you receive. If you consider this option, make sure to include the difference in expenditures of the two living arrangements (utilities, property and other taxes, transportation, etc.).
- If you do not have a lump sum of money to invest, consider buying into a mutual fund a little at a time each month. Most mutual funds require only a small initial deposit if you sign up for automatic contributions. The monthly contributions will add up to big savings over time.

But before you select any investment fund, do the research to find out about charges, length of contract and hidden fees. If you do your homework, you will avoid surprise charges and disappointing earnings.

The Resources

www.aarp.org

American Association Retired Persons Website.

www.dol.gov/dol/topic/retirement/index.htm

Good information available at the Retirement Plans area of the U.S. Department of Labor's Website.

www.asec.org

American Savings Education Council Website provides useful savings tips.

www.money.cnn.com

Several good articles on CNN's Money Website.

www.nefe.org

The National Endowment for Financial Education® (NEFE®) is a non-profit 501(c)(3) foundation dedicated to helping all Americans acquire the information and gain the skills necessary to take control of their personal finances.

www.bloomberg.com/analysis/calculaotrs/retire.html

Bloomberg's Website provides several interactive retirement calculators.

www.choosetosave.org/

Choose to Save® Website includes a variety of helpful savings and retirement calculators.

When to
Start Saving

The Challenge

At what age should you start saving for retirement? Financial planners will tell you it is never too early to start saving money towards retirement, and starting as early as your teen years is optimal.

Although you cannot open a retirement account until you reach 18, you do not need to open an IRA to start saving for retirement at any age. For example, take a look at one family who put away half of their 12-year old daughter's earnings into a custodial savings account to be earmarked for a future retirement account. When $1,000 accumulated in the saving account the money was transferred into a money market account. Once she reached the age of 18 and was old enough to open an IRA account, the money was deposited into the account. Needless to say the daughter was none too happy, knowing she could not touch this portion of her earnings for another 50 years, until she understood that the initial $1,000 would grow to $19,935.95 (at a 6 percent growth rate) by the time she retires at age 68. If she contributes $1,000 a year for the next 4 years the account will grow to more than $70,000 when she reaches full retirement age. And to illustrate the point further, if she put away $3,190.51 each year until retirement she would have $1 million in savings by age 68. All of a sudden mom and dad were not looking so bad.

This example illustrates the importance of starting a savings account early and letting the money grow over a longer period of time. It is never too late to start saving for retirement but as the following examples show, sooner builds faster than later.

The Facts

Start young is the advice of retirement planners. The earlier you start saving the more interest you will earn and the less likely it is you will have to play catch-up as you get closer to retirement age. Delaying starting a savings plan or postponing contributing to your plan can have a huge impact on your results. A delay of even a few years can cost you thousands of dollars.

Here is an example of how postponing your savings plan can really cost you in the long run:

If you save $200 a month for 10 years at a 6 percent return you will net $32,653. However, if you delay your savings plan by just 2 years, you will net only $24,519. That 2-year delay will cost you $8,134.

The longer you postpone contributing to your saving plan the bigger the difference will be. Thus, postponing your savings plan by 10 years could end up costing you $32,653 in earned interest.

Not only will the delay in creating a savings plan cost you lost interest, it will also force you to contribute more on an annual basis to achieve the same results.

Look at it from a different perspective: If you wish to save $500,000 over a period of 40 years, starting at age 25 you will need to put away $329.69 per month, assuming a conservative 5 percent return on investment. At the end of the 40 years you will have earned $343,527 in interest from a principal investment of $158,251, for a total savings of $501,778.

Now, look at it from the opposite perspective: By postponing contributions to your savings plan for 10 years, but still putting away $329.69 per month (assuming the same conservative 5 percent return on investment), at the end of 30 years you will have earned $157,286 in interest from your principal investment of $118,688 to give you a total net amount of $275,974. The 10-year delay has cost you $225,804!

Years	Annual Contributions	Principal	Interest = 5%	Total
40 years	$ 3,956.28	$ 158,251	$ 343,527	$ 501,778
30 years	$ 3,956.28	$ 118,688	$ 157,286	$ 275,974
Difference:	$ 0.0	-$ 39,563	-$186,241	-$225,804

The Solution

The key to developing a successful retirement plan is to start your planning at an early age, determine what you need to contribute to reach your goals and make regular contributions. Then, set a monthly contribution amount that you can live with. It is better to make smaller contributions on a regular basis than larger, less frequent deposits. Smaller contributions made regularly will produce higher returns. Consider starting out with a contribution amount of only $1,000 a year.

This will equal about $20 a week. Pay yourself first by signing up for automatic deductions from your paycheck. Another strategy is to reinvest your tax refunds into your retirement account. Instituting small steps like these will make it easier to invest on a regular basis versus planning a lump sum payment that may be difficult to produce and easy to skip.

Finally, plan to increase your contributions as your income grows. Start out by contributing 10 (or even 1) percent of your income and gradually increase it a couple of percentage points every 5 years. This will help increase your principal amount and offset the effects of inflation at the same time.

The Resources

www.lfg.com/LincolnPageServer?LFGPage=/lfg/ipc/index.html

Lincoln Financial Group's tools section includes financial calculators to help guide you with your financial planning activities.

www.principal.com/calculators/retire.htm

Principal.com Website offers savings calculators and numerous articles on social security and retirement planning.

www.defenselink.mil/militarypay/retirement/calc/index.html

Office of Secretary of Defense Website offers information and calculators about military retirement choices.

www.fundadvice.com/tools/calculators

Retirement and investment calculators to help you make mutual fund, retirement and active risk management decisions.

www.choosetosave.org/calculators

ASEC is a national coalition of public and private sector institutions committed to making saving and retirement planning a priority for all Americans.

www.math.com/students/calculators/source/compound.htm

Math.com provides compound interest calculators so you can see how compounding interest benefits your retirement savings. Math.com provides ways for students, parents, teachers, and *everyone* to learn math.

What You Must Save to Maintain Your Current Income

The Challenge

How much money will you need to retire? Pick a number, any number, and then double or even triple it! Extended life spans, reduced employer benefits, lower market returns and increased living costs are forcing us to save more.

According to a recent study conducted by The Employee Benefits Research Institute (EBRI), the proportion of workers saving for retirement is seven in 10 (or 70 percent). This is an encouraging number. Yet, those who report they have attempted to calculate their savings needs to maintain their current income during retirement is only 42 percent. This means that while 70 percent of those surveyed are saving, only 42 percent know how much they need to save! The EBRI also reports that if current trends continue, by 2030 the annual shortfall between the amount needed during retirement and the amount actually saved will be at least $45 billion.

Saving any amount for retirement is a good start, but you need to know if you are saving enough. If you want to avoid working until you reach 80, calculate now how much you will need in the future and create a plan to get you there.

The Facts

Nearly one-quarter (24 percent) of workers surveyed by EBRI are very confident about their financial security during retirement, while more than four in 10 (44 percent) are somewhat confident. However, those who say they are very confident may in fact be overconfident.

- Twenty-two percent of very confident workers are not currently saving for retirement.
- Thirty-nine percent have less than $50,000 in savings.
- Thirty-seven percent have not yet done a retirement needs calculation.

These are rather scary statistics and it is easy to poke fun of everyone else. But let me ask you this–have you done a retirement needs calculation? Do you know how much to save to maintain your current income post retirement? Why not?

This table shows you how much you need to save to maintain your current level of income.

Annual Retirement Income Need	Total Nest Egg Required (Estimate)
$50,000	$833,333
$100,000	$1,666,667
$175,000	$2,916,667
$250,000	$4,166,667

Keep in mind that the above table is based on a rough formula. When calculating your target nest egg and how much you have to save each month to reach that target, there are many factors that come into play:

- your current age
- life expectancy
- income sources during retirement
- expected savings contributions
- portfolio risk/return
- intended retirement age
- current earnings
- amount of current retirement savings
- cash outflows during retirement
- rate of inflation

Incorporating some of these factors, the following table illustrates how much you need to save each month to realize a $1 million savings. The table assumes that your annual investment rate of return on your savings is 8 percent (which of course, cannot be guaranteed).

Number of Years Left Until Retirement	Monthly Amount Required to Save (to attain $1 million goal)*
35	$435.94
30	$670.98
25	$1,051.50
20	$1,697.73
15	$2,889.85
10	$5,466.09

*Assuming an 8 percent Rate of Return

Clearly, planning for retirement is not something you should put off until shortly before you stop working. Because of the magic of compounding, the earlier you start a retirement plan, the less you have to save on a monthly basis—as illustrated in the table above. Other factors, such as a lower interest rate or higher inflation, will require a much higher contribution.

The table below shows how much you need to save if you started with a savings base of $25,000 while earning a lower interest rate of only 5 percent instead of 8 percent.

Age	Savings base	Amt. monthly to become a millionaire at 65	Interest rate
25	$25,000	$ 539.97	5%
35	$25,000	$1,071.72	5%
45	$25,000	$2,271.00	5%

As you can see, planning for retirement is a lifelong process where time is truly on your side. Throughout all your working years, you should make it a habit to review your plans to evaluate your progress and target goals and to make adjustment necessary to ensure you reach your goals.

The Solution

Now you know how much you need to save if you want to be a millionaire at age 65. If you did not start saving at age 21, you may find it difficult to save the necessary $2,300 a month at age 45 just as you are paying for college tuitions, weddings or home care for an aging parent. Maybe the $1 million amount is not realistic for you. What is your magic number? The worksheet below will help you determine exactly how much you will need to save to supplement other retirement income.

Annual income from Social Security	
Man's age 65	$ _____
Woman's age 65	$ _____
Annual Income from Pensions and Employer Benefits	
Company name	$ _____
State or federal government	$ _____
Veteran's	$ _____
Union or other	$ _____
Profit-sharing	$ _____
Deferred pay	$ _____
Other	$ _____
Annual Income from Savings and Investments	
IRA	$ _____
Savings account (interest)	$ _____
Money market (interest)	$ _____
Treasury securities (interest)	$ _____
Mutual funds (dividends, capital gains)	$ _____
Stocks (dividends)	$ _____
Bonds (interest)	$ _____
Real estate (rent)	$ _____
Farm/business rent or Installment payments	$ _____
Home equity conversion	$ _____
Annuities	$ _____
Other	$ _____

Earnings	
Salary, wages	$ _____
Commissions, royalties, fees	$ _____
Partnership income	$ _____
Assets which could be liquidated	
Real Estate	$ _____
Mutual Funds	$ _____
Stocks	$ _____
Bonds	$ _____
Antiques, collectibles	$ _____
Farm/Business	$ _____
Anticipated gift or inheritance	$ _____
Possible deductions from income	
Federal income tax	$ _____
State/city income tax	$ _____
Social Security tax	$ _____
Total Retirement Income	
Amount needed to maintain pre-retirement income:	$ _____
Shortfall/Excess	$ _____

1. First, using the worksheet above, add up all the rows to get your Total Retirement Income.
2. Next, take your current income and multiply it by .70 to determine how much you will need to replace 70 percent of your income.

The difference between your estimated total income and amount needed to maintain your pre-retirement income is the shortfall or gap you will be left with.

The point being made here is that as important as it is to save, savings alone are not enough. You also need to invest wisely (see Chapter 9: *Allocate Your Assets*). Planning may seem daunting, but it just requires discipline, dedication, determination and, most importantly, time.

It has been said that most people spend more time planning their annual vacation than they spend planning their retirement. If you spent a little more time planning your retirement, think about all the travel you can plan when you retire!

The Resources

www.nefe.org/latesavers/partone.html

Interactive Website dedicated to helping people save for retirement.

www.choosetosave.org/calculators

ASEC is a national coalition of public and private sector institutions committed to making saving and retirement planning a priority for all Americans. ASEC is a program of the Employee Benefit Research Institute Education and Research Fund (EBRI-ERF), a 501(c)3 non-profit organization *www.ebri.org*

7

Factor in
Inflation

The Challenge

With inflation running at only about 4 percent over the last century, it is easy to dismiss how it will affect your overall savings plan 15 or 25 years from now. But inflation is something you should not ignore and hope goes away. Just like compounding, the cumulative impact of even low rates of inflation over time can have a substantial effect on your investments. In any case, inflation can substantially erode your savings.

As an example, say you have a savings account at your local bank paying 3 percent interest annually. If you have set aside $2,500 a year for 25 years, you will have saved $62,500 of your own money, which, at 3 percent, would grow to $92,900 during that same period. Now, factor in 4 percent annual inflation and, although your grand total is the same, the value of your investment drops to the equivalent of only $55,575 after inflation. That is a big bite out of your spending power!

All this is not meant to discourage you, but to enlighten you. Inflation is inevitable and if you pay attention, you can plan for it and adjust your savings plans to minimize the erosion and even come out ahead. Understanding the effects of inflation on your long-term plans will help you create a saving and investing plan that counteracts inflation. A good rule of thumb is to annually add in additional reserves to offset the cost of inflation. Your challenge is to keep track of the rate of inflation each year and take action to preserve your savings.

The Facts

A simplified definition of the word inflation is an increase in the price you pay or a decline in the purchasing power of money. In other words, price inflation is when prices get higher or when it takes more money to buy the same item. The Bureau of Labor Statistics in the United States measures inflation using the Consumer Price Index (CPI).

Explaining the CPI gets a little technical, but it is important background information you need to understand. The CPI is a price index published by the U.S. Bureau of Labor Statistics on a monthly basis. You may have heard it called the cost-of-living index. This index attempts to track the change in prices of the typical group of goods and services consumed by an average family of four with a median income. Each monthly survey taken determines the weighting of the chosen representative prices for successive refinements in the computation of the price index. The so-called market basket, covered by the index, includes items such as food, clothing, automobiles, homes and fees to doctors.

The CPI fluctuates from month to month as does inflation. History provides a summary of inflation rates by decade to reveal some of the reasons why rising inflation correlates to major economic and social events, such as the crash of 1929, World War II and the recession years in the 1970s.

Year	Averaged Rate of Inflation
1914–1919	14.57%
1920–1929	0%
1930–1939	-1.42%
1940–1949	-1.24%
1950–1959	.69%
1960–1969	5.46%
1970–1979	11.35%
1980–1989	4.82%
1990–1999	2.24%
2000–2006	2.75%

Source: www.inflationdata.com

The Solution

Keeping abreast of annual inflation rates and taking steps to adjust your retirement savings plan to compensate for inflation will mean more spending power and fewer surprises when it is time to retire. Taking steps to minimize inflation are easy.

First, calculate the annual rate of inflation by looking up the CPI at your local library or visiting the Bureau of Labor Statistics Website at *www.bls.gov*. Once you know the CPI you can calculate the rate of inflation to determine just how much adjustment you may need to make to your annual retirement plan contributions.

The formula for calculating the inflation rate using the CPI is fairly easy. For example, each month the Bureau of Labor Statistics (BLS) surveys prices and generates the current Consumer Price Index. Image for a minute that the BLS in 1994 published the index at 100. By today's prices, the same item that cost $1.00 in 1994 might now cost $1.90, so that index would now stand at 190. At first glance the increase went from 100 to 190, but how much did it really increase?

To calculate the change, take the second number (190) and subtract the first number (100). The result is 90. Now we know that since 1994 prices have inflated by 90 points. To convert the 90 points to a percentage, multiply the first price of 100 by the current price (190) to get .90. Next multiply .90 by 100 to see there has been a 90 percent increase in the CPI since 1994. Now you can use this number to determine a specific inflation rate.

Calculating a Specific Inflation Rate

The method of calculating inflation is the same, regardless of the time period. We just substitute a different value for the first one. If you want to know how much prices have increased during the last 12 months you simply subtract last year's index from the current index and divide by last year's number, multiply the result by 100 and add a percent sign. Sounds easy enough. Here it is in formula form.

The formula for calculating the inflation rate is:

$$((Current\ index)\ B-A\ (last\ year's\ index))/A(last\ year's\ index))*100$$

The formula may be easier to understand using actual figures. If one year ago the CPI was 175 and today it is 185, the calculation would look like this:

$$((185-175)/185)*100 = 5.41\ or\ (10/185)*100 = 5.41\ or\ 0.0514*100 = 5.41\%$$

Thus, the inflation rate is 5.41 percent over the sample year. Armed with this information you can minimize the rate of inflation by increasing the amount of money you allocate to your retirement plan for the year by 5 percent. Thus, if you are currently contributing $1,000 per month towards a 401(k) or other retirement account, to offset inflation you would increase your contribution by $50.

If prices go down, then it is referred to as a price deflation. This results in A being larger than B and you would end up with a negative number. So, if last year's CPI was 189 and this year it went down to 180, then the formula would look like this:

$$((180-189)/189)*100 = -.476\ or\ (-9/189)*100 = -.476\ or\ -.0476.*100 = -4.76$$

This shows a negative 4.76 percent inflation over during the year. A negative result is not called inflation but deflation.

Keeping track of the future value of your investments will help you more accurately project your retirement income. Obviously the closer you are to retirement the less likely inflation will eat away at your savings. But if you are still decades away from reaching your retirement age, keep track of the annual rate of inflation and take steps to head off any nasty surprises. Regardless of whether inflation is running into the double digits or deflation occurs, knowing in advance will keep your retirement plans on track.

Once you know how inflation affects your investments you can control how much money to put away based on inflation. Use your rate of inflation calculation to your planning advantage by pairing it with the Rule of 72.

The Rule of 72 is a rule of thumb that will help you compute when your money will double at any given interest rate. The rule earned its name because at 10 percent, money will double every 7.2 years. Interestingly enough, the calculation is accurate at any interest rate, not just 10 percent.

To use this simple rule, divide 72 by the annual interest rate. For example, if you are getting a 6 percent rate of return on an investment and that rate is constant, you money will double in 12 years.

72 divided by 6 = 12 years

The Rule of 72 when the rate of return is known

If you know you can earn 5 percent on your money, you may want to know how long it will take to double your money at this rate of return. Using the Rule of 72 simply divide 72 by the rate of return (in this case 5 percent). The answer is it would take 14.3 years to double the investment.

The Rule of 72 when the number of years is known

The rule of 72 can also be used to determine the rate you would have to earn to double your money in a certain number of years. For example, if you wanted to double your money in 4 years you would divide 72 by four. The calculation shows you would need an 18 percent compounded return in order to double your money in 4 years.

The Resources

http://stats.bls.gov/

> The U.S. Department of Labor, Bureau of Statistics provides current inflation and consumer price index figures.

www.inflationdata.com

> Published by the Financial Trend Forecaster, InflationData.com provides the most current inflation rate data on the Web, in addition to information on the other monetary activities of the Federal Government and US Treasury.

8

The Time Value
of Money

The Challenge

A dollar is a dollar. It will be worth the same 100 pennies next year as it is today. In theory this is correct, in practice, it is not. We have seen how, through inflation, the value of a dollar can be worth less in the future than it is worth today. The time value of money is the relationship between time and money. According to the present value of money concept, a dollar earned today is worth more than a dollar earned in the future. How can that be? Through the time value of money. Time value refers to the belief that a dollar in hand today is worth more than a dollar promised at some future time.

Consider this: If you receive $10,000 today you can manage your money two ways, you can increase the future value of your money by investing and gaining interest over a period of time or you can leave the money sitting in a non-interest bearing checking account. If you leave it in the non-interest checking account you are losing the income you could have been earning if you had put it into an interest-bearing account. If you let money earn interest, your initial investment will grow over time and time equals greater value.

The trade-off between money now and money later depends on, among other things, the rate of interest you can earn by investing. This chapter provides explains the formulas you can use to calculate simple and compound interest to determine the time value of your money.

The Facts

You can say that the future value of the dollar is $1.06 given a 6 percent interest rate and a 1-year period. It follows that the present value of the $1.06 you expect to receive in 1 year is only $1.

What will be the future value of your money? The answer depends on if your money is earning simple or compound interest.

Simple Interest

Calculating simple interest is the easiest of the future value formulas. If you invest $10,000 in a simple interest account at 5 percent interest, the future value of your money at the end of the first year will $10,500. To determine the simple interest multiply, the principal amount of $10,000 by the interest rate of 5 percent and then add the interest gained to the principal amount. The future value of your savings at end of first year will be:

Present value + (present value * 5%) = future value or
$10,000 + ($10,000 * .05) = $10,500

Keep in mind that simple interest is calculated only on the initial principal. For instance, if someone were to receive 5 percent interest on a beginning value of $10,000, the first year interest would be:

.05 x $10,000 = $500

If you continued to receive 5 percent interest on the original $10,000 amount, over 5 years the simple interest growth in your investment would equal:

Year 1: 5% of $10,000 = $500 + $10,000 = $10,500
Year 2: 5% of $10,000 = $500 + $10,500 = $11,000
Year 3: 5% of $10,000 = $500 + $11,000 = $11,500
Year 4: 5% of $10,000 = $500 + $11,500 = $12,000
Year 5: 5% of $10,000 = $500 + $12,000 = $12,500

The interest earned would remain the same $500 from year to year.

Compound Interest

Compound interest is the interest you earn on the principal amount you invest and on the accumulated interest earned in previous periods. The difference between compounding interest and simple interest is with compounding interest you are earning interest on interest where with simple interest you are earning interest only on the principal. Compound interest is usually used in most time-value-of-money calculations

For example, if you invest $25 a week for 10 years starting at age 25 at an annual return of 4 percent, you will have $135,000 by age 70, even though you only invested $12,000 of your own money. By investing your savings and leaving it untouched, your interest continues to earn interest each year until you retire. For example: if you receive 5 percent compound interest on a beginning value of $10,000, the first year they would get the same thing as if they were receiving simple interest on the $10,0000, or $500. The second year, though, the interest would be calculated on the beginning amount in year 2, which would be $10,500. So their interest would be:

.05 x $10,500 or $525 in compounded interest

Therefore, you balance at the end of the 2nd year would be $11,025. Five years of compounding interest would look like:

Year 1: 5% of $100 = $500.00 + $10,000.00 = $10,500.00
Year 2: 5% of $100 = $525.00 + $10,500.00 = $11,025.00
Year 3: 5% of $100 = $551.25 + $11,025.00 = $11,576.25
Year 3: 5% of $100 = $578.81 + $11,576.25 = $12,155.06
Year 4: 5% of $100 = $607.76 + $12,155.06 = $12,762.82

Compounding interest will obviously earn you more money from your initial investment. The future value of a $10,000 investment in 5 years, at a 5 percent compound rate would be $12,762.82 or $262.82 more than you would have earned at a simple interest rate.

This table summarizes the future value factors for various interest rates by year. To use the table, simply go down the left-hand column to locate the appropriate number of years. Then go out along the top row until the appropriate interest rate is located.

For instance, to find the future value of $100 at 5 percent compound interest, look up 5 years on the table then go across to 5 percent interest. At the intersection of these two values, a factor of 1.2763 appears.

Multiply the 1.2763 factor times the beginning value of $10,000 to view the results: $1,276.30. With rounding up this is the number that was calculated using the Compound Interest Formula above.

Future Value Factors							
Period in Years	Interest Rate 1%	Interest Rate 2%	Interest Rate 3%	Interest Rate 4%	Interest Rate 5%	Interest Rate 6%	Interest Rate 7%
1	1.0100	1.0200	1.0300	1.0400	1.0500	1.0600	1.0700
2	1.0201	1.0404	1.0609	1.0816	1.1025	1.1236	1.1449
3	1.0303	1.0612	1.0927	1.1249	1.1576	1.1910	1.2250
4	1.0406	1.0824	1.1255	1.1699	1.2155	1.2625	1.3108
5	1.0510	1.1041	1.1593	1.2167	1.2763	1.3382	1.4026
6	1.0615	1.1262	1.1941	1.2653	1.3401	1.4185	1.5007
7	1.0721	1.1487	1.2299	1.3159	1.4071	1.5036	1.6058
8	1.0829	1.1717	1.2668	1.3686	1.4775	1.5938	1.7182
9	1.0937	1.1951	1.3048	1.4233	1.5513	1.6895	1.8385
10	1.1046	1.2190	1.3439	1.4802	1.6289	1.7908	1.9672
11	1.1157	1.2434	1.3842	1.5395	1.7103	1.8983	2.1049
12	1.1268	1.2682	1.4258	1.6010	1.7959	2.0122	2.2522
13	1.1381	1.2936	1.4685	1.6651	1.8856	2.1329	2.4098
14	1.1495	1.3195	1.5126	1.7317	1.9799	2.2609	2.5785

Present Value

You can go calculate the present value of money simple by working the formula backwards.

If you were promised $10,000 in 5 years. How much money would I have to give you now to make up for lost interest as a result of the delay of payment?

For example, the formula to determine the present value using the exponential might look like this: FV= Future Value, PV=Present Value, i=interest rate, N=number of years.

$$FV = PV (1 + i)^N$$
$$\$10,000 = PV (1 + .05)^5$$
$$\$10,000 = PV (1.340)$$
$$\$10,000 / 1.340 = PV$$
$$\$7,462.69 = PV$$

Therefore if you give me $ 7,462.69 today and in 5 years I will give you $10,000. You will have earned a 5 percent interest on your money.

The Solution

The concept of the time value of money underscores the many options you have to invest your money. Using the time value calculations will forecast the proposed return on investment for many different investment vehicles. This tool is especially helpful for determining the future value of annuities.

These present value and future value calculations demonstrate that time is money-the value of the money you have now is not the same as it will be in the future and vice versa. So, it is important to know how to calculate the time value of money so that you can distinguish between the worth of investments that offer you returns at different times.

The Resources

www.studyfinance.com/lessons/timevalue/index.mv?page=04

Studyfinance.com's overview about time value of money. This website offers a terrific overview about how to compute the future value of money. Includes interactive worksheets and tables.

http://teachmefinance.com/timevalueofmoney.html

TeachMeFinance.com teaches you basic finance concept

9

Create Your Investment Profile–Allocate Your Assets

The Challenge

What type of investor are you? Do you enjoy taking risks or are you more cautious? Identifying your investor comfort zone will dictate how you allocate your money to meet your goals.

If you are a:

- Risk-adverse or conservative investor who is close to retirement, you may look for investments with guaranteed rates of return that will protect your investment.
- Moderate investor who understands that a little risk over the long-term will generate higher returns, you have time on your side and losses will be offset by gains over the long haul.
- Aggressive investor and thrive on the ups and downs of the stock market, you are willing to accept high volatility for the chance to grow your assets substantially.

Regardless of what type of investor you are, you should tailor your plan to meet your financial goals. Your first step to defining your goals is to create an investment strategy and define your investment objectives.

- What are your financial goals at retirement?
- How will you get there? Do you want to protect your money, grow it or earn income from it?
- What is your timeline? Different timeframes require different strategies.
- Which investments have the best potential to meet your goals.
- What could sidetrack your savings plan? Identify all the risks that could prevent you from reaching your goals?

Once you define your objects then you can choose your strategy.

The Facts

There are three main strategies involved in investing:

1. Protect your money.
2. Earn income from your money.
3. Grow your money.

Protecting your money means keeping it in the safest investment possible. Market fluctuations are avoided so the principal remains untouched no matter how much the return may go up or down. An example of an investment strategy that protects you money is putting it into a savings account or certificate of deposit. The principal will not grow very quickly and may actually be outpaced by inflation, but you will not lose a penny of the principal.

Earning income from your money means you want a regular, predictable stream of income from your investments. One common method to earn income from your money may be to invest it in bonds or mutual funds, thereby earning income from the interest payments. In this instance your money is making you money.

Another strategy is to invest in stocks or stock funds that invest in stocks that pay dividends. The best strategy would be to evaluate your income/growth needs, and probably employ some combination of the above. There are also products available that will guarantee minimum amounts of income for life.

Growing your money may mean investing smaller amounts of money in different stocks or mutual funds. Over time, as the value builds or grows, you could sell your shares that increase in value for a profit.

The Solution

Aggressive investors buy stocks for growth, moderate investors buy bonds for income, while safe investors keep cash or buy money market securities. You can divide your money between each type of investment based on your individual goals and risk-aversion comfort level. Over the long-term, a diversified mix of investments can outperform a very conservative investment in money market securities or Treasury bills, and at the same time avoid the higher risk of an all-stock portfolio. Asset allocation, which involves selecting the balance of stocks, bonds and cash equivalents, is the key to creating a high performing portfolio.

Financial experts agree that a proper balance of asset allocation accounts for about 90 percent of all investment success. Focusing more on investing in the correct categories and focusing less on a single investment area such as stocks or bonds will help you achieve this success. Your plan does not have to be perfect from the beginning and may need adjusting from time to time. In fact, it should change as your risk levels will change as you grow older.

Here is a look at how portfolios traditionally might have been allocated for investors with various retirement ages:

If Retirement is	Stocks	Bonds	Cash
20-30 years away	80%	15%	5%
10-20 years away	60%	30%	10%
5 years away	40%	40%	20%
Today	30% or less	40-80%	20% or more

These are typical allocations, but as people are living much longer these days, and as life expectancy continues to rise, more and more financial professionals agree, that even at retirement, a fair amount of your portfolio needs to be invested in growth. The more you have in growth, the better your chances are of not outliving your income. Growth also hedges against inflation. This presents a whole new set of challenges for the next generation of retirees. A proper investment allocation becomes increasingly important, during theses times of increasing life expectancy. You still need growth, but your tolerance for risk is diminished.

Of course, when you are planning to retire and how much income you will need in retirement is an important consideration in determining your asset mix, since the longer you plan to invest the money, the more risk you can afford to take. Spread your portfolio between aggressive and conservative investments. Conservative or safe investments include bonds, CDs, mutual funds and savings accounts. The closer you are to retirement the more money you should allocate into safe investments. Your returns will be smaller but your investment will be protected. If your retirement date is further away investing your money in more aggressive funds will likely yield greater returns.

At least once a year you should take time to evaluate your portfolio with an eye to adjusting your mix of stocks, bonds, and cash to maintain the return on investment percentages you are comfortable with.

The Risk Ladder

Highest Risk/Higher Return Potential
> Stocks, Options, Futures, Collectibles

Medium Risk/Return Potential
> Real Estate, Mutual Funds, Small Cap Companies, Mid Cap Companies, Large Cap Companies

Lowest Risk/Lower Return Potential

High-Income Bonds. Government Bonds, Money Market, Certificates of Deposit, Cash and Cash Equivalents

How you invest your assets depends primarily on two things: (1) how much risk you can put up with and (2) how close you are to retirement.

Suggested Asset Allocations by Age and Risk:

Age Range	No Risk	Medium Risk	High Risk
40s	0	55%	45%
50s	10%	60%	30%
60s	35%	45%	20%
70s	60%	30%	10%

How much equity is appropriate for your age? Although every situation is different, there is one time-tested formula that can help you arrive at the right amount of equities (stocks, stock mutual funds and real estate) in your portfolio for your investment age: the percentage of equities equals 110 percent minus your age.

For example, as a rule of thumb, if you are 55 years old you would have 110 minus 55 or 55 percent of your investment in equities. If you have $500,000 in investments by age 55 you would allocate 55 percent or more of your investments in real estate, stocks or mutual funds for a total of $275,000.

The Resources

http://apps.nasd.com/invesstor_Information/Tools/Calculators/ retirement_calc.asp

The home page for investors on the Internet offers a number of tips and resources.

www.investorhome.com/process.htm

Determine how long your retirement savings will last.

www.financeCalc.com

Free retirement planner calculators.

www.morningstar.com

Investing tools and calculators to solve your specific investment strategy.

10

Your Investment—
ROI, ROA, ROE

The Challenge

It is not enough to just put money into a retirement account and forget about it for
the next 20 years. We have all heard the cries from financial planners stating that if
you had put away $1,000 a year in a balanced portfolio since 1963 you would now
have a million dollars in your retirement fund. Global economies and business
structures change over time and these changes should also influence how closely
you monitor your investments over time.

This chapter reviews the more technical side of investing—measuring results.
The casual investor may find this chapter tedious and too technical, but we have
included it because every investor should be provided the same tools professional
financial planners use to measure performance. Return on investment (ROI),
return on equity (ROE) and return on assets (ROA) provide you with three
different performance tracking tools—each with their own purpose.

In this chapter we will review the uses and benefits of each formula.

The Facts

Your portfolio is made up various investments. Each investment performs
differently from year to year. In order to track the individual performance of each
investment you can use an return on investment (ROI) calculator. The calculator
enables you to measure the performance of one investment relative to another.
ROI is presented as a percentage and is based on returns over a specific period to
time, usually one year. This calculator keeps track of your investment returns and
lets you determine if you need to make changes.

Another tool to help you determine if you need to make portfolio changes is the
return on equity (ROE) calculator. ROE is an important ratio that shows how
effectively a company is managing investors' money. It shows whether or not
management is growing the company's value at an acceptable rate. This ratio is

very useful if you have funds invested with a money manager or investment firm. You can use this ratio to compare how well your individual investment portfolio stacks up to an investment company's portfolio. Use this calculator before selecting an investment group to invest your money for you.

The third tool to use to decide whether to make portfolio changes is the return on assets (ROA). This return calculation offers a different view on management's effectiveness and reveals how much profit a company earns for every dollar of its assets. Assets include things like cash in the bank, accounts receiveable, property, equipment, inventory and furniture. This calculation is very helpful to help you determine the financial health of a company before you invest. Use this calculation before selecting stocks and corporate bonds. A declining ROA is a telltale sign that trouble is around the corner, especially for growth companies.

The Solution

Astute planners monitor each of their investments annually and make adjustments in order to keep their financial goals on track. If, after analysis, an investment is returning lower than expected (or needed) results, changes may be made. It is very important to arm yourself with the tools you will need to evaluate your current and future investments.

ROI Calculation

1. Record the amount of your total investment, including fees and expenses. For example, if you bought $1,000 worth of stock and your fees were $50 then your total investment is $1,000 + $50 = $1,050.
2. Next, record your net profit or loss from the investment for the year. If your $1,050 investment in stocks (including any dividends) increased to $1,300 during a 12-month period then your profit is $1,300 - $1,050 = $250.
3. Finally, calculate the ROI by dividing the profit by the total investment. A $250 profit would yield a 19.5 percent ROI ($250/$1,050 =.195 or 19.5 percent).

ROI can be calculated for a year, a month, a week or a day. For example, if a $200 investment returns $100 after one month, then the monthly ROI would be a 50 percent profit ($100 profit divided by $200 investment = .50 or 50 percent.)

ROE Calculation

Another useful calculation is return on equity, which shows how effectively a company is managing shareholders' money. ROE is calculated by dividing the annual net income by the average shareholder equity. You can find net income and shareholder equity reported in the company prospectus or annual report.

For example: In 2005, a company reported a net income of $15 million and total stockholder equity of $10 million. In 2004 total stockholder equity was $7 million. To calculate the ROE, first find the average of the shareholder equity for the two years ($10 million + $7 million divided by 2 = $8.5 million). Then, divide the net income for 2005 ($15 million) by the average shareholder equity ($8.5 million). This is your ROE ($15 million/$8.5 million = .57 or 57 percent) or profit of every dollar invested.

ROA Calculation

Return on assets gauges how efficiently a company can earn a profit from its assets. A company's assets include cash in the bank, accounts receivables, property, equipment, inventory and furniture. The simplest way to determine ROA is to take net income reported for a period and divide that by total assets (annual net income/total assets). To get total assets, calculate the average of the beginning and ending asset values for the same time period. Using the numbers above, divide the income earned in 2005 ($15 million) by the amount of assets reported on the annual report ($350 million). In this case, the return on assets is $15 million/$350 million or .04 or 4 percent profit against the assets it owns. A high ROA is a positive sign of solid financial and operational performance. An ROA of 20 percent means the company produces $1 profit for every $5 invested in assets.

ROA provides investors with a reliable picture of management's ability to produce profits from the assets and its own investments.

By making good use of all three analyses tools, ROI, ROE and ROA, you can quickly recognize how well a company is managed, identify good stock opportunities and minimize surprises in your investments. How often you monitor your investments is a personal choice. However, experts agree that monitoring your investments too often can cause an investor to prematurely alter a potentially successful investment strategy; they recommend you measure investment performance using any one of these tools on a semi- or annual basis only.

The Resources

www.investopedia.com

Investopedia.com provides a dictionary, articles, tutorials, stock ideas, research, retirement information and various calculators for the novice or experienced investor, and for active traders.

www.pine-grove.com/financial%20calculators/roi.htm

This calculator calculates both the annualized rate of return on an investment liquidated on a specified date and the gross rate of return.

www.dinkytown.net/java/InvestmentReturn.html

This calculator helps you sort through these factors and determine your bottom line. Calculate your investment capital and rate of return, inflation, taxes and your time horizon.

http://beginnersinvest.about.com/cs/investinglessions/1/blreturnonasset.htm

About.com Investing Lesson #4–article about return on assets.

www.webcalc.net/calc/business/1052.php

WebCalc, is a web-based calculator with currently 400 different calculations available with more being added daily.

www.credit-to-cash-advisor.com/document_120.html

Credit-to-cash advisor offers one of the easiest ways to gauge whether a company is an asset creator or a cash consumer by providing a return on equity (ROE) calculator. The Dupont Analysis is a means of analyzing the three components of return on equity.

11

What Retirement Age
Is Right for Me?

The Challenge

A secure, comfortable retirement is every worker's dream. Now that we are living longer, healthier lives we can expect to spend more time in retirement than our parents did. Achieving the dream of a secure, comfortable retirement is possible if you take time to plan your finances.

Your retirement plan is the foundation on which you can build a secure retirement. Most financial advisors say you will need between 70 percent to 75 percent of your pre-retirement earnings to comfortably maintain your pre-retirement standard of living. Currently, if you have average earnings, your Social Security retirement benefits will replace only about 40 percent and you will need to supplement your benefits with a pension, savings or other investments. (The percentage Social Security will replace is lower for people in the upper income brackets and higher for people with low incomes.) Social Security was never intended to replace your full income upon retirement; it is only intended to fill the gaps.

It was not too long ago when the stock market was riding high and it was not a question of if you will retire but how early you would retire. Many people relied heavily on the rising stock market to fulfill their desire of retiring at age 55 when poof! their dreams quickly turned to disbelief as the stock market spiraled downward taking profits and often entire investments down with it. Workers who envisioned themselves weeks away from retirement are still working hard today, years later, to bring their retirement funds back to sustainable levels.

An integral part of any retirement plan is deciding when is the right time to retire. It is not just a matter of picking a future date; it is also knowing you will be financially and mentally prepared for retirement. Other considerations you should review before selecting a retirement date include:

- Determining the annual income you will need to meet your future financial obligations and where that income will come from.
- Creating a portfolio diverse enough to remain stable during economic ups and downs.
- Factoring in any unexpected expenses between now and retirement such as housing repairs, medical bills or high inflation rates.
- Planning your post-retirement life.

The Facts

Choosing a retirement date is dependent on how you will meet your financial obligations at a reduced income rate. When you stop working, your paychecks stop too. How will you earn the 70 percent you need to maintain your lifestyle? You can start collecting Social Security retirement benefits as early as age 62, but the amount you will receive will be less than your full retirement benefit amount. Retirement before normal retirement age (NRA) reduces benefits, and retirement after NRA increases benefits.

If you start your benefits early, they will be permanently reduced based on the number of months you receive benefits before you reach your full retirement age. For example, if you were born after 1937, you can start receiving your retirement benefits at age 62, but the reduction in your benefit amount depends on your year of birth. The maximum reduction at age 62 will be:

- Twenty-five percent for people who reach age 62 in 2005.
- Thirty percent for people born after 1959.

Putting this into dollars, if you begin collecting your benefits today at age 62, your monthly benefit amount will be $824.00. If you wait to collect benefits until you are 65, your monthly benefit amount will increase to $1,058.00. If you wait to collect benefits until you are 70, your monthly benefit amount increases to $1,327.00.

The monthly benefit is lower the earlier you retire. The monthly difference is based on the calculation that you will be receiving benefits for three or more years than someone aged 65 or 70 who waits to collect.

Can you meet all your financial obligations on the reduced benefit amount? If you are expecting to live on a monthly $2,000 budget, do you have the resources to make up the $1,200 difference each month for the rest of your life? Of course, you should also factor in inflation in future years. What $2,000 will buy you today will not be the same in 10 years.

The Solution

Before entering retirement, take a realistic look at your financial retirement future to make sure that your new lifestyle will fit the image you have planned. A good dose of realistic planning is the best defense to making a common mistake of overspending during the early years of retirement. Remember, the faster you reduce the principal in your retirement account the less you have in future years.

Forecasting how much money you will need for retirement is a difficult exercise. It is very easy to foresee big expenses today and it is even easier to forget to add something in especially 10 or 20 years from today. You may already have a couple of retirement dates picked out. How realistic have you been in your planning to make one of those dates a reality? To determine if you can really retire at your target date, you can project future expenses and compare them with projected income.

To provide a rough estimate of future expenses, create a spreadsheet that contains expenses by year. Expand the worksheet by each year to meet your life expectancy. (Use 85 years as your life expectancy.) An assumption factored into this worksheet is housing costs at a fixed-rate (meaning you will not be buying a new or more expensive home during retirement). A second assumption is you will continue to pay down a mortgage. If you plan on paying off a mortgage during this time period or if you plan to purchase a replacement home or condo, adjust your living expenses to reflect the change.

- In the first column list all projected expenses.
- In the top of each column across the spreadsheet include each year in chronological order.
- On the bottom of each column tally your total expenses,
- Estimate your tax rate for each year (.15 minus 1.0 = .85)
- Multiply your total expenses times your tax rate to estimate how much retirement income you will need each year.

To help determine your projected retirement expenses, fill out the *Projected Expenses Worksheet* located at *www.encouragementpress.com*

How do your projected expenses measure up to your expected retirement income?

Regardless of when you plan to retire, create a portfolio diverse enough to remain stable during economic ups and downs that will cover your costs.

Do not let your lifestyle outpace your retirement income. Before you retire, plan how you will create a paycheck from a combination of Social Security, your assets and other resources. A common complaint from retirees is that they regret not having paid more attention to how they would replace their retirement income.

Be sure to factor in any unexpected expenses such as housing repairs, medical bills or high inflation rates. It is also a good idea to continue to put money into a separate savings account to create a reserve fund to cover increased medical costs and higher inflation.

Retirement for many is downright boring. After working a structured day for so many years, not knowing what you will do with your free time could be a challenge. Consider what you will do with your days. If you plan to travel or go back to school you will need to include extra money into your budget. Many retirees enjoy both travel and continuing their education by attending Elderhostel's around the world.

If you decide to teach or start a new career then you will need to add the influx of income back into your planning projections. Additional income will also affect your benefits.

Check out how much money you will receive in benefits each month by using the Social Security Benefits calculator. This handy calculator helps you project your benefits in today's dollars and inflated dollars. Visit *www.socialsecurity.gov/OACT/quickcalc/* to review your benefits based on your birth date and a pre-populated estimated earnings history. You may improve the calculator's accuracy by entering in actual income information provided on your Social Security Statement.

According to the Employee Benefit Research Institute, nearly four in 10 workers say they want to retire before age 65. Do not be too anxious to leave work. Studies have shown that older retirees are much happier in retirement than younger retirees. And if you can manage it, staying even a few extra years can dramatically improve your finances.

The Resources

Several good income and retirement benefit calculators are available on the Web.

www.cnnmoney.com

Provides a retirement planner.

www.tiaa-cref.com

Download a budget worksheet. Look in the Turning Savings into Retirement Income area in the Retirement Countdown section of the TIAA-CREF Website.

www3.troweprice.com/ric/RIC

Use T. Rowe Price's retirement income calculator to see how long your money might last.

www.ssa.gov

Social Security Online, to calculate various retirement age scenarios.

12

So Many Retirement Plans To Choose...

The Challenge

Everyone has different needs and preferences when choosing a retirement plan. There are several kinds of structured, or qualified or tax deferred, retirement plans that will help you achieve your financial goals while providing tax incentives for you to regularly fund your plans. As you continue to build a diversified portfolio, you may also investigate and invest in different unqualified, or taxed, investment plans.

With a qualified plan you postpone or defer paying taxes on your contributions and on your investment earnings until you begin to withdraw the money, which may be as early as 59½. Your employer often offers qualified plans, and contributions to the plan may be tax deductible. These are also known as salary reduction plans as your money is deposited into your account pre-tax. The more money you put into your defined plan, the lower your taxable salary and the less taxes you pay. These types of plans include 401(k), 403(b) and 457 plans. In order for an employer and the employee to deduct contributions to a qualified plan, it must meet the following requirements:

- The plan must be written.
- The plan must be established with an infinite timeline–no expiration date.
- A custodian must hold in trust the plan assets.
- The plan must be established by a registered company and not by an individual.
- The plan must provide a specific period during which participants vest in their retirement accounts.

With an unqualified plan, you have to pay taxes on the money before you invest it, essentially leaving you less to invest. Examples of unqualified investment vehicles include insurance plans, such as annuities and stocks and bonds. The advantage to both qualified and non-qualified plans is that the interest remains tax-deferred until you start taking it out after retirement.

Familiarizing yourself with each type of plan can be challenging. If you have a qualified plan through your employer, it is a good idea to at least familiarize yourself with the basics of that particular plan. Such as, when will you be vested?, how much is your employer contributing?, when can you take distributions? In this chapter we will take a look at the different types of retirement plans and their requirements.

The Facts

Employer plans are those plans that can only be established by an employer on behalf of the employees. These plans allow you to take a tax deduction for contributions to the plan. Employer plans include SIMPLE IRA, SEP, Profit Sharing 401(k), and defined plans such as pension plans. Individual plans are those that you can establish for yourself as an individual.

Qualified Plans

IRA

Individual retirement accounts (IRAs) are tax-deferred personal retirement plans. There are two types of traditional IRAs, deductible and non-deductible, and Roth. All traditional IRAs are tax-deferred accounts. That means you owe no tax on your earnings until you withdraw money. A traditional IRA is established by an individual and not by a business. You may open a traditional IRA regardless of how high your income is or what other types of plans you have in place if:

- You (or, if you file a joint return, your spouse) received taxable compensation during the year, and
- You will not be age 70½ by the end of the year.

You are able to deduct your annual contributions if you and your spouse are not participating in any other qualified retirement plans or, even if you or your spouse participated in another qualified play, your earned income was below the threshold amount for the year as defined by the IRS. However, you cannot contribute more than you earn.

Personal Retirement Savings Plans

Personal retirement savings plans are also known as IRAs, or individual retirement accounts. Although there is a surprisingly large variety of them, they can be generally categorized as the traditional IRA and the Roth IRA. Principal and interest accumulations in both types and are untaxed until they are withdrawn. One difference between the two types has to do with tax-deductibility. Whether or not contributions to a traditional IRA are deductible in the year they are made depends on several things, including the owner's tax filing status and adjusted gross income. Even if only one spouse is working, both can have an IRA. And if one spouse is covered by a traditional retirement plan and the other works but is not, the second spouse may make a tax-deductible contribution to an IRA.

ESOPs

Employee stock ownership plans, which strictly speaking are defined contribution plans, are funded by contributions of company stock to the plan, usually allocated according to each participant's salary. Often, employees may also buy additional shares to add to the plan. Dividends from stock in the account are added to the account.

Profit Sharing

Easier and more flexible than a 401(k) plan, profit sharing allows the employer to allocate contributions among employee accounts–they do not have to be distributed equally. If employers want to reward long-term employees and exclude short-timers, it can. Employees can contribute the maximum percentage (as mandated by the IRS) of their net self-employment earnings each year and can contribute a different percentage each year.

401(k)

401(k)s allow you to contribute untaxed funds (tax-deferred) directly from your paycheck into a 401(k) account, so instead of the employer, you are funding your own pension. You do not pay taxes on the income until you start withdrawing it. The employer may also choose to contribute a percentage of what you contribute, so long as it is the same percentage for all employees. In addition, 401(k) plans sometimes have a profit-sharing component that applies to the employer's contribution. Although you cannot withdraw assets completely without paying a penalty, and you cannot use them as security for other loans, you can borrow from the funds for certain emergencies or expenses, such as the down payment on a house, medical bills or to further your education. You must pay the loan back with interest within a specific period of time, but you are paying yourself back with interest.

SEP

Small companies, as well as self-employed people, partnerships, sole proprietors and independent contractors may set up simplified employee pensions (SEP) without the hassle and expense of running a qualified retirement plan. (Companies may not have both SEPs and qualified plans.) The employer may contribute to the plan to individual retirement accounts for each employee. Only employees named have access to the funds, though they are subject the IRA rules. If you have your own business, contributions to your SEP are tax-deductible. The plans may be structured like either a 401(k) or an IRA. The employer must make a matching contribution of up to 3 percent of the employee's pay, but may reducethe maximum percentage in any 2 years out of 5.

Roth IRA

Like traditional IRAs, Roth IRAs are individual plans, not employer plans. Contributions to a Roth are made after taxes (you have already paid taxes on the money) and contributions cannot be deducted from taxes. If you are married and have a combined adjusted income of $170,000 or more you cannot make any contribution to a Roth IRA. The big attraction to a Roth IRA is when you start taking distribution after age 59½ the interest and capital gains you earn inside the Roth and all future contributions are mostly tax-free. Another difference between the Roth and the traditional IRA is the manner in which they are taxed when you begin taking withdrawals. In a Roth you are allowed to take all distributions tax-free. Because you did not deduct your contributions, it is made with after-tax dollars. The bonus here is that you are not taxed on your contributions, only the interest earned are taxed. In a traditional IRA your entire withdrawal is taxed (including the earnings) when you begin to take withdrawals.

Simple IRA

If your net earnings from self-employment are $40,000 or less and are not likely to increase, you might be interested in a SIMPLE IRA plan. It is easy to set up and can be set up anytime during the year. You will not need to file a tax return for the SIMPLE IRA even if the assets grow to a large sum.

The Solution

The type of retirement plan that is best for you is a balanced and diversified portfolio that is distributed equally between tax-deferred and taxed plans. Retirement plans are living, breathing entities. Plan requirements, maximum contribution amounts and age restrictions change each year and may be difficult to keep up with. Visit our Website *www.encouragementpress.com* to view a complete Planning Comparison Chart summarizing the components of each type of plan.

The Resources

www.irs.gov/publications/p590/ar01.html

> IRS *Publication 590* reviews individual retirement arrangements.

www.irs.gov/pub/irs-pdf/p560.pdf

> IRS *Publication 560* reviews retirement plans for small business.

www.dol.gov/dol/topic/retirement/index.htm

> The U.S. Department of Labor explains retirement plans, benefits and savings.

13

Mutual Funds: Front-Loaded & No-Load Funds

The Challenge

More than 80 million people in America have more than $6 trillion invested in mutual funds. Mutual funds have been around since the 1920s, yet their popularity over the past 25 years has soared. The reasons: Mutual funds are easy for the individual investor to manage and can produce a higher rate of return. Mutual funds also bring diversification and professional money management to the individual investor.

A mutual fund pools the money of many investors (called shareholders) to invest in a variety of different securities. Securities may be in stocks, bonds, money market securities, real estate or a combination of all. Investors share in any profits or losses when the securities are sold. For the individual investor, mutual funds provide the benefit of having someone else manage your investments, including account recordkeeping, and diversifying your dollars between many securities that typically would not be available or affordable to you otherwise. Minimum investment requirements on many funds today are low enough that even the smallest investor can get started in mutual funds.

Mutual funds play an important role in balancing out a retirement portfolio. Understanding the terminology, the different types of funds and the fees associated with each fund is important when deciding which fund to join.

The Facts

There are different types of mutual funds with different objectives and various levels of growth potential. Some mutual funds specialize in narrowly defined areas, such as real estate, or purchase stocks only within a specific industry. Other funds represent a large group of stocks, such as the whole stock market or just small or large company stocks. These types of funds are referred to as index funds as the fund buys stocks in the same proportion as a particular index. The most popular index fund is the S&P 500 Index. This fund includes stock from 500 companies.

There are also money market mutual funds. This type of account is similar to a savings account but, because of the large amount of money combined into one account, investors earn a higher interest rate.

Load vs. No-Load

There are two basic kinds of mutual funds—load and no-load. They are different only in the way they are sold. A load fund pays a commission to a sales person, financial planner or broker when you buy into the fund. A no-load fund does not involve salespeople or brokers. You deal directly with the mutual fund company. Since there is no commission to pay, there is no load.

The advantage of a load fund is that you receive professional advice on which fund to choose. The disadvantage is that the commission you pay reduces your initial investment into the fund. Both types of funds typically charge an annual management fee that may be as low as .10 percent or as high as 2 percent.

Share Classes of Mutual Funds

Different types of funds, or share classes, have different charges to cover the cost for any advice you receive in selecting the fund. Each share class has different sales charges, or loads, and different fee structures. Basic definitions of share classes include:

A Shares

Typically called load funds and offered through brokers, these funds are sold with an initial, or front-end sales charge (usually 3 percent to 6 percent) that is deducted from your initial investment. Also, these funds most always charge a 12b-1 marketing fee that is deducted from the fund's assets each year. Breakpoints are generally offered on A share purchases. This means that the larger the lump sum you invest, the lower your up-front sales charge is. An example of a breakpoint would be a stock fund that charges 5.7 percent up front if you invest up to $50,000. If you invest $50,000 to $99,999 you would be charged 4.5 percent, and so on. Typically bond funds, charge lower sales charges then stock funds. Look in the individual funds prospectus for information on your specific fund.

B Shares

These funds have no front-end sales charge, but carry a redemption fee, or back-end load that you pay if you redeem shares within a certain number of years. This load (called a contingent deferred sales charge or CDSC) declines every year until it disappears—usually after 6 years. B share funds also carry a 12b-1 marketing fee that is typically higher than the 12b-1 fee of A shares. After the time period ends, some funds will convert B shares to A shares so your fees are reduced. Due to many brokers misrepresenting these funds as no-load, many fund companies have discontinued B shares.

C Shares

Known as a level-load share, C shares have no front-end sales charge and no redemption fee, but they carry a 12b-1 marketing fee that you pay for as long as you hold the fund. It is similar to no-load funds that charge 12b-1 fees.

D Shares

D Share are variations of the three basic classes.

1. Management Fees and Operating Expenses.
   All mutual funds, regardless of the type, have management fees and operating expenses for maintaining records and sending shareholder reports. Fees are reflected in the fund's share price and are not charged directly to the shareholder. The management fee usually ranges from 0.5 percent to 1 percent of the fund's total asset value, but may be higher for specialized funds.
2. 12b-1 Fee.
   A 12b-1 fee permits a fund to pay some or all of the costs of distributing its shares to the public. Specific expenses such as advertising, sales literature and sales incentives may be paid out of plan fees. Charges are fully explained in the fund's prospectus. For a fund to be called no-load, its 12b-1 fee must not exceed 0.25% of assets.
3. Redemption Fees.
   A fee is charged when you redeem (sell) or exchange your shares for shares of another fund from the same company. This can be a simple fee at redemption, or an exchange fee or a CDSC. A redemption fee is often returned to the fund itself, rather than to the management company. A CDSC, sometimes called a back-end load, goes to the management company to pay sales commissions.

The Solution

Once you have identified your goals and the types of funds available to help you reach them, the next step is to identify specific funds that will be most suitable for you and learn more about them before you make your investment.

Mutual fund rates of return fluctuate with market conditions, changes in the valuation of the securities a fund invests in, or other factors. For that reason, you need to do your homework before investing by comparing the performance of several funds. Be sure that you are making accurate comparisons: compare funds with the same investment objectives and fund policies before you look at the numbers. Remember when comparing results of a load fund to a no-load fund, adjust performance results to include the load or redemption fee for a more accurate evaluation. The way to compare funds is to look at:

Average Annual Total Return which is defined as the percentage change in a fund's net asset value, or share price, over a specified time. It takes into account the impact of any distributions, dividends and interest payments and assumes reinvestment of all income dividends and capital gains distributions.

Assume the current value of shares you own is currently worth $6,500.

1. Take the current value of shares ($6,500) and subtract the original investment ($5,000). This will give you the increase in value ($1,500).
2. Take the increase in value ($1,500) and add the capital gains, dividends or interest distributions paid ($500) to get your profit ($2,000).
3. Take your profit($2,000), divide it by the original investment ($5,000), and multiply by 100 to get your total return (40 percent for the 2-year period).

Yield is a measure of a fund's dividend income or earnings paid out to you, usually expressed as a percentage of its current share price over a designated period. For a mutual fund, yield consists of dividend payments divided by the beginning value of the fund's shares (before any gain or loss in the price per share).

As with any investment, careful analysis of past performance and thorough study of current market trends are essential to selecting the right fund for you. Using these tools and the resource calculators offered through the SEC and NASD will help you select the best investment for you. Always review the prospectus carefully before investing.

The Resources

www.irs.gov

IRS *Publication 564* discusses mutual fund distributions and IRS *Publication 550* discusses investment income and expenses.

http://apps.nasd.com/investor_Information/ea/nasd/mfetf.aspx

This site contains the NASD Mutual Fund Expense Analyzer. At this site, the NASD compares the fees and expenses of up to three mutual funds, or the share classes of the same mutual fund on the NASD's Mutual Fund Expense Analyzer.

Additional resources are provided in Chapter 50 under Mutual Funds.

14
Riding the Stock Market

The Challenge

Stock owners will tell you that everyday feels like they are riding a roller coaster–some days there is exhilaration as the stocks rise, and other days there is anxiety as the stocks drop. The stock market is full of risks, and if you have the stomach for the highs and lows the risks can be very rewarding.

Since the 1950s the average market investor earned an annual return of 13 percent compared to a steady 6 percent for cash and bond investments. Keep in mind, however, the 13 percent return covers 50 years of market ups and downs. The stock market can be extremely volatile and in any give year can climb quickly and fall fast (you may remember black Tuesday in 1989 and the rapidly climbing and tumbling values of 2000 and 2001).

A balanced portfolio is a productive portfolio. In order to build a balanced portfolio, it is important to understand the stock market, different types of stocks and how to weigh your portfolio based on your age to maximize your return. This chapter will provide you with a brief overview and key points to consider when purchasing stocks.

The Facts

Buying stock in a company means you have paid for an individual ownership interest (or share) in the company. If you purchase 100 shares in a company that has 10,000 shares outstanding, then you own 1 percent of that company's net worth.

There are two ways investors can make money on stocks:

Dividends

> A taxable payout to shareholders, usually given in cash but may also take the form of stock or other property. Companies are not required to pay dividends. Some companies prefer to reinvest a dividend back into the company to increase its overall value.

Gains
> Proceeds from the sale of stock that increased in value from the day it was purchased until the day it was sold. (If you choose to sell the stock you will only have to pay taxes at the more favorable capital gains rate if you have owned it for at least one year.)

A stock's price will have something to do with the financial success of the company but it is also independently affected by:

- What is going on in the national and global economy;
- consumer demand for the stock;
- how the stocks of other companies in the market are doing; and
- the expectations of investors about economic growth, interest rates and taxes and other intangible factors such as consumer confidence.

Companies may issue two types of stocks:

Common stock is the most commonly issued form of stock.
> This type of stock provides the shareholder with a greater voice with the company as it contains voting rights. Shareholders, however, are also exposed to greater risks, especially if the company goes out of business or files for bankruptcy. In that case, common stockholders are paid only after all other creditors are paid.

Preferred stock is a mix between regular common stock and a bond.
> Each share of preferred stock is usually paid a guaranteed dividend. In the event of bankruptcy, preferred shareholders have greater rights to a company's assets than common stockholders. However, preferred stock owners generally do not have voting privileges.

> Preferred stock generates predictable income–often twice that of common stock. However, common stock is more volatile and can gain a higher value faster. Preferred stocks are recommended for people approaching or in retirement that are looking for a fixed income.

Other common terms you should know are:

Buying on margin
> This allows you to put down just half the price and borrow the rest from the stockbroker and using the stock as security.

Selling short
> This means you are selling shares you do not own on the speculation that you will make money if the share price goes down after you buy. You can double your money when you sell short, but the amount you can lose is infinite.

The Solution

When you invest in stocks, be clear about your investment goals, especially your long-term goals. The two most important factors to consider when creating your investment plan are how much risk are you comfortable taking and when will you need access to your money. Other important stock tips include:

- Factor in all the tax implications of buying and selling stocks. Be aware of transaction or trading fees you will pay even if you sell at a loss.
- Diversify your stock portfolio. You can decrease your risk by owning a variety of types of securities in a variety of industries. You can increase your diversity by investing in mutual funds.
- Consider whether to change investments to correspond to the amount of risk you can bear at different ages. Younger investors might aim for long-term growth with a little higher risk. Workers nearing retirement may look for investments with less growth but more stability. Spreading investment risks evenly will help keep the portfolio balanced and you will achieve greater growth.
- A different mixture of small cap, growth and international stocks will change a low risk investment into a high-risk investment. Keep in mind a low risk investment may yield a lower rate of return.

Sample Asset Allocations			
	Low Risk	**Medium Risk**	**High Risk**
Small cap stocks	0%	15%	0%
Growth stocks	30%	30%	65%
International	10%	10%	10%
Bonds	30%	35%	15%
Treasury bills	30%	10%	10%

Remember, there is no magic formula to help you pick stocks to invest. Your goals should help guide you in looking for the right combination and types of stocks in which to invest.

Before selecting a company stock to purchase, review:

- The company's cash flow statement;
- net profit stated earnings report;
- sales—both gross and net and countries and companies the product is being sold to;
- net and gross earnings;
- the ratio of profit to total assets;
- the competitiveness of the company's products; and
- changes in the preceding factors from year to year.

You can get much of this information from company annual reports and Websites, such as *www.edgaronline.gov* (the SEC site) and from market research services like Morningstar, usually found in a public library.

If you are interested in investing in stocks, here are 10 tips to help you get started:

1. Select a handful of likely stock prospects within a specific industry.
2. Read copies of a company's annual report and 10K filing (an SEC quarterly financial statement).
3. Compare multi-year financial data from the company's annual report.
4. Determine if a company is growing by dividing the current-year revenue (gross sales) by the gross sales for the previous year and subtracting one from the result. You will then see whether sales are really growing.
5. Review how much long-term debt the company has compared with its assets. Look at the company's Statement of Operations to see how it is spending its money.
6. Review the company's return on assets (ROA) that you can calculate by taking total earnings divided by total assets.
7. Analyze the current price to earnings ratio (P/E) and compare it to the company's past ratios.
8. Check to ensure the company is increasing sales from year to year.
9. Verify that the company is bringing in enough cash to cover operating expenses and overhead.
10. Look to see how reasonably the stock is priced. You can do this by looking at the P/E ratio. If a stock sells for $60 and is earning $5 a share, it has a P/E ratio of $12. The stock is considered a good buy if the P/E ratio is at or below the annual rate of the company's earnings. For example, if the company's profits are growing by 20 percent to 25 percent, a company that usually has a P/E of 15 may still be a good buy at a P/E of 20.

Investing in stocks is not like investing in an annuity, mutual fund or individual retirement account. Stock values are much more volatile and can change rapidly. The more sophisticated investor may be more comfortable owning individual stocks, while a novice stock investor may be less comfortable and choose to reduce his or her risk by owning stocks through a stock mutual fund. Your financial advisor or stockbroker will be able to explain the best stock options for your risk level and to create a balanced portfolio to meet your future financial goals.

The Resources

Additional stock Websites include:

- *www.morningstar.com* (Morningstar)
- *http://wsj.com/public/us* (Wall Street Journal)
- *www.bloomberg.com* (Bloomberg)
- *www.money.cnn/com/markerts* (CNNMoney)

The Advantage of Annuities

15

The Challenge

An annuity is defined as a contract between an individual and a life insurance company that guarantees periodic payments to the owner or beneficiary during a specific period. Annuities allow you to accumulate tax-deferred funds for retirement and then, if you desire, receive a guaranteed income (this process is called annuitization) payable for life or for a specified period of time, generally a term of 5 or 10 years thereby spreading out your tax-burden and providing income security.

Annuities can be categorized in two different ways. First an annuity may be either immediate or deferred. Second, an annuity may be either variable or fixed.

Annuities offer three primary advantages: 1) they are tax deferred; 2) probate can be avoided; and 3) income can be guaranteed for a period of time or for life.

The Facts

Since the 1970s, annuities have become a popular addition to retirement planning. Depending on your age and your level of comfort, you may select an annuity that is secure and risk-free (fixed) or one that carries more risk but may produce greater returns, such as an equity indexed or variable annuity fund. The different types of annuities include:

Fixed Annuities
> The fixed-rate annuity is very similar to a bank certificate of deposit, but typically pays a higher minimum interest rate and offer greater security. A fixed interest rate is guaranteed and you will receive this amount regardless of market trends. Fixed annuities are secure and safe, no-risk investments, which make them popular with conservative investors and for those who want to be guaranteed an exact return on their investment.

Equity Indexed Annuities (EIAs)
> An EIA is a variation of a fixed-rate annuity. As with a fixed annuity, you are guaranteed to receive a minimum interest rate. However, the

rate of return is determined by a formula based on changes in the index to which the annuity is linked. The formula decides if and how any additional interest is calculated and credited. An equity-indexed annuity's interest rate is linked to such indices as Standard & Poor's 500 Composite Stock Price Index (S&P 500). Review contract terms carefully for they may include long surrender periods and many loopholes.

Variable Annuities

Variable annuities provide flexibility, allowing you to invest simultaneously across a wide array of securities, such as bonds, mutual funds, stocks, futures, etc. You may invest the annuity premium any way you want, but there are greater risks with this type of annuity along with the opportunity for greater returns. If the securities the annuity is based upon increase 20 percent, you keep all gains. Consequently, if the investment drops 20 percent you absorb the loss. Variable annuities are best for the more aggressive investor who desires investment flexibility, although there are variable annuities that offer riders that will guarantee your principal and/or a minimum amount of income over your lifetime.

An annuity payout may either be immediate or deferred.

Immediate Annuities

An immediate annuity generally involves a lump-sum payment resulting in a stream of income. You purchase this type of annuity with one payment and must begin receiving income payments within 12 months. An immediate annuity could help secure your retirement by locking in a guaranteed income stream. You choose the payout period, which may be a lifetime income option that you cannot outlive. With an immediate annuity, you can set the amount of your initial monthly annuity income payment. You can also choose a period certain, which guarantees payout over a certain period of time.

Deferred Annuities

A deferred annuity allows you to defer your income payments and to accumulate money on a tax-deferred basis for long-term goals such as retirement, and may be purchased by making either a single payment or a series of payments. When you are ready to receive income from your annuity, you can withdraw funds as needed, or you can set up a regular annuity income payment schedule that would last for life or over a given time period in the same manner as immediate annuities.

Period Certain Only Annuities

This type of annuitiy guarantees level payments for a defined time period (5, 10, 15 or 20 years). If you should die before the end of the certain period, payments will be paid to your designated beneficiary. No payments are made to the annuitant after the end of the specified period.

If you die, a person you select as a beneficiary, such as your spouse or child, will receive the greater of either all the money in your account or some guaranteed minimum (such as all purchase payments minus prior withdrawals).

Fees and Charges

Annuities may include charges and fees. Be sure you understand all the charges before you invest. These charges will reduce the value of your account and the return on your investment. Always ask for a detail listing of all charges that may apply or a schedule of fees. Fees may include:

- Surrender charges.
- Mortality and expense risk charge.
- Administrative fees.
- Underlying fund expenses.
- Fees and charges for other features.

The Solution

Flexibility, security and risk aversion are some of the general advantages of annuities. The right choice depends upon your current needs and your investment portfolio.

Do not be afraid to ask questions and jot down the answers, so you can compare your options. Before you decide to buy a variable annuity, consider the following questions:

- Are you willing to take a risk with a variable rate annuity or is a fixed-rate annuity a better choice for you?
- Do you understand the features of the annuity?
- Do you understand all of the fees and expenses that the annuity charges?
- Do you intend to remain in the annuity long enough to avoid paying any surrender charges if you have to withdraw money?
- Are there features of the annuity, such as long-term care insurance, that you could purchase?
- Have you consulted with a tax adviser and considered all the tax consequences of purchasing an annuity, including the effect of annuity payments on your tax status in retirement?

Fixed deferred annuities make sense if you:

- Desire the security and safety of a guaranteed interest rate;
- want tax deferral advantages;
- have considerable assets to set aside for at least five years;
- are looking to potentially convert into a future income; and
- are saving for retirement.

Variable annuities make sense if you:

- Want gains of potential market growth;
- have significant assets to set aside for 10 years or more;
- want tax deferral advantages;
- are looking to potentially convert into a future income; and
- are saving for retirement.

Immediate income annuities make sense if you:

- Are in retirement or are entering retirement;
- desire a guaranteed retirement income;
- have a rollover or lump sum to convert into an income stream; and
- have concerns about outliving your income.

To decide what option best fits your unique requirements it is best to consult a licensed agent to analyze your current circumstances, portfolio and financial needs.

The Resources

www.annuity.com

Annuity.com educates investors about annuities and puts them in touch with quality agents to help them decide if an annuity is right for them.

www.annuityadvantage.com

This site lists and compares more than 300 fixed and CD-type annuities ranked by highest yield to surrender. It also provides tax information and calculators.

www.sec.gov

The U.S. Securities and Exchange Commission site provides helpful resources and online publications.

www.nasd.com

NASD is an independent self-regulatory organization charged with regulating the securities industry, including sellers of variable annuities.

www.naic.org

The National Association of Insurance Commissioners Website contains a wide variety of resources.

16

Fixed vs. Variable Annuities

The Challenge

Although not a new investment strategy, the inclusion of annuities into a balanced retirement plan has gained wider acceptance. Annuities can be purchased through a broker or insurance agent with a lump sum payment or in installments. Annuities are most suitable for investors between 40 and 59 who are interested in sheltering money from taxes before retirement.

Not all annuities are created equal and, therefore, they are not right for every investment situation. Fixed-rate and variable rate annuities provide different benefits to each investor, operate under different fee structures and may produce vastly different results. Like every investment, it is important to understand the risks and rewards before you incorporate annuities into your investment portfolio.

The Facts

Fixed Annuities

The fixed-rate annuity is very similar to a bank CD, but typically pays a higher minimum interest rate and offers greater security. A fixed interest rate is guaranteed and you will receive this amount regardless of market trends. Fixed annuities are secure and safe no-risk investments, which make them popular with conservative investors and for those who want to be guaranteed an exact return on their investment.

Equity indexed annuities (EIAs) are a variation of a fixed-rate annuities. As with a fixed annuity, you are guaranteed to receive a minimum interest rate. However, the rate of return is determined by a formula based on changes in the index to which the annuity is linked. The formula decides if and how any additional interest is calculated and credited. An equity-indexed annuity's interest rate is linked to such indices as Standard & Poor's 500 Composite Stock Price Index (S&P 500). Regardless of the index performance, you are guaranteed to retain all of your initial principle if an EIA contract is held for a minimum period of time.

Variable Annuities

Variable annuities operate more like a mutual fund, providing flexibility by allowing you to allocate your assets among a variety of options, such as bonds, mutual funds, stocks, futures, etc. You may invest the annuity premium any way you want, but there are greater risks with this type of annuity. Variable annuities do not guarantee a fixed-rate of return. If the annuity value increases 20 percent, you keep all gains; if the investment drops 20 percent, you absorb the loss. A variable annuity is a popular investment choice for the more aggressive investor who desires investment flexibility.

The comparison between a fixed and variable annuity:

	Fixed-Rate	Variable Rate
Return on investment	• Guaranteed fixed interest rate of return. • Investments are often in the form of government securities, mortgage securities and CDs. • Provides more security of principal.	• Rate of return is not guaranteed so return rate may vary. • Investments are often in the form of stocks, bonds, treasuries, zeros coupon bonds and real estate. • More risk but potentially higher returns.
Tax issues	• Interest earned is not taxed until money is withdrawn then will be taxed at ordinary income rates (can run as high as 35%). • If money is withdrawn before 59½ you pay income tax and a 10% penalty. • Early withdrawal penalty if money is taken out within first 7 to 10 years.	• Interest earned is not taxed until money is withdrawn then will be taxed at ordinary income rates (can run as high as 35%). • If money is withdrawn before 59½ you pay income tax and a 10% penalty. • Early withdrawal penalty if money is taken out within first 7 to 10 years.
Investment options	• Investment options and allocation selected and managed by the issuing insurance company.	• Investor allocates funds. Funding options include mutual funds, stocks and bonds. • Annuities purchased with after-tax dollars lets you transfer money to different funds without paying taxes on the earnings. • Investment categories are outlined in an investment prospectus.
Risks	• Conservative investment. • No risk of loss. • Guaranteed return rate.	• Riskier investment. Investor may lose some or all principal and interest. • Return rate is not guaranteed.
Insured	• Not insured by the Federal Deposit Insurance Corporation (FDIC) although is backed by the insurance company/industry.	• Not insured by the Federal Deposit Insurance Corporation (FDIC) although is backed by the insurance company/industry.

Fees	• Maintenance and contract fee of $25 to $50 per year. • Insurer expense of 1 to 1.5% of the assets. • Average .3 to 1% advisor fee on the assets. • Surrender fee of 5% to 8% if annuity is closed before 10-year term is complete.	• Maintenance and contract fee of $25 to $50 per year. • Insurer expense of 1 to 1.5% of the assets. • Average .3 to 1% advisor fee on the assets. • Surrender charges 5% to 8% if annuity is closed before 10-year term is complete. • M&E (mortality & expense) charge may be 2% a year. • Management and fund operating fee (includes fund manager's salary and prospectus costs).
Commissions	• Sales commission of 4% to 8.5%.	• Sales commission of 4% to 8.5%.

The Solution

Think carefully about the fees, risks and returns of investing in annuities before purchasing. Investing in an annuity is a good choice for certain age groups and not for others. If you are considering purchasing an annuity, compare returns against mutual funds and certificate of deposits (CDs). If you are between 40 and 59, an annuity may be the best investment option; if you are in your 20s or 30s, an annuity would be considered a poor investment choice. Selecting the right investment for your age and goals is important to maximizing returns and minimizing taxes. Investigate all investment options thoroughly before you invest.

Research Fees

Before investing in an annuity, understand all the fees and charges associated with variable and fixed-rate annuities. As indicated earlier, variable rate annuities charge higher fees to manage and maintain an account. Make sure that these high fees do not end up eating away your profit and possibly your principal too.

Read the Prospectus

For a variable annuity, important information will be explained in the prospectus that describes the variable annuity contract. The prospectus must be given to you when you are considering the purchase of a contract with after-tax dollars.

A prospectus is created for every variable rate annuity and provides the historic performance of the fund, fund allocation, costs, expenses and the risks associated with investing in the fund. Read the prospects in its entirety before investing. If you have questions do not be fearful of asking the investment advisor. Remember, annuities, like stocks and bonds, are commission-based.

Hybrid Annuities

If you are uncomfortable with the volatility of variable annuities but want a better return than a fixed annuity will guarantee, seek out a hybrid variable annuity that combines characteristics from both the variable and fixed-rate products. Some variable annuities offer a range of investment options and a fixed account option that guarantees both principal and interest, just like a fixed annuity. You are given the option of dividing your money between the low-risk fixed option and higher-risk vehicles such as stocks or equity-indexed annuities, all under the umbrella of just one annuity. Many variable annuities offer asset allocation programs to help you decide where to invest your assets based on your circumstances.

Annuities offer some unique advantages over other investments. As with all investments you must take the time to understand how annuities work. Research how they operate, their costs and the advantages and disadvantages to investing in different kinds of annuities. This way you will be prepared for the fees and risks associated with annuities as an investment tool.

The Resources

www.annuityadvantage.com/equityindexed.htm

> The Annuity Advantage Website offers an article explaining equity-indexed annuities.

www.annuity.com

> Annuity.com educates investors about annuities and puts them in touch with quality agents to help them decide if an annuity is right for them.

www.annuityadvantage.com

> This site lists and compares more than 300 fixed and CD-type annuities ranked by highest yield to surrender. It also provides tax information and calculators.

www.sec.gov

> The U.S. Securities and Exchange Commission site provides helpful resources and online publications.

www.nasd.com

> NASD is an independent self-regulatory organization charged with regulating the securities industry, including sellers of variable annuities.

www.naic.org

> The official Website for the National Association of Insurance Commissioners has various resources on annuities.

17
Savings Accounts & CDs

The Challenge

The closer to retirement you are, the more conservative your investment strategy will become. At this stage of the game you want to preserve the investments you have built-up over the years and not take any chances that your hard-earned dollars might be lost to changing markets. This is the time you have been saving for and having access to your money is a must. Beginning at age 70½, you must start taking required minimum distributions whether you need the money or not.

The challenge becomes where to park this money for the short-term while making it work for you. A few options include a savings account, certificates of deposit (CD) or money market funds. If you shop carefully, you will find that any one of these options can offer interest rates almost as high as a fixed-rate annuity or 401(k) plan.

The Facts

How much interest you can earn depends on your own lifestyle. If you need cash at hand at all times, then a savings account is probably the best solution for you. If you do not mind tying up your money for a few months, then putting your money into a CD may be a good solution. Or perhaps a money market account is best. Your money earns a higher interest rate and you are able to withdraw money from the account six times a month without penalty. Again, each account type has its advantages and disadvantages. The facts will help you decide which option is best for you.

Savings Accounts
- A savings account will generate the smallest return on your investment.
- Interest is calculated on a fixed annual yield rate.
- Interest is taxable.
- A small minimum balance is required to open an account.
- There are no deposit and withdrawal requirements or restrictions.

- Deposits are guaranteed by FDIC/FSLIC insurance up to $100,000 per account ($250,000 for IRAs).
- Your money is accessible any time.
- Interest rates are set by each individual bank and may be different at each bank. Some may offer rates as low as one-half percent while an online bank may offer rates as high as 4.80 percent.

Certificates of Deposit (CDs)

Long-term CDs are ideal for investing toward the purchase of a big-ticket item such as a car or vacation. A good first step for beginning investors is to move some of your funds from your savings or checking account to a CD.

- CDs pay a fixed-rate of interest that is tied to the length of the contract term. The longer the term the higher the interest rate.
- Interest earned is taxable.
- Money is accessible and may be withdrawn, but you will be charged a penalty. Some banks require you forfeit the entire interest earned, some will only charge a month's interest and some will charge you only for the interest on the funds withdrawn.
- Deposits are guaranteed by Federal Deposit Insurance Corporation/Federal Savings & Loan Insurance Corporation (FDIC/FSLIC) insurance up to $100,000 per account.
- Upon maturity you may choose to have the CD automatically rollover into another CD or move it to another investment vehicle like a bond or mutual fund.

Money Markets

Money market funds are suitable for conservative investors who want high stability of principal and moderate current income with immediate liquidity. There are two types of money markets: money market fund and money market account.

Money Market Fund (MMF)

- A money market fund is a type of mutual fund that must invest in low-risk securities. Money market funds typically invest in government securities, certificates of deposits, commercial paper of companies and other highly liquid and low-risk securities (not usually stocks).
- Shareholders invest money (called shares). Each share is valued at a Net Asset Value (NAV) of $1 per share. The NAV is constant and does not change; only the dividend yield may change.
- If the money market performs poorly and the NAV falls below $1, the investor will lose money.
- Earnings, in the form of dividends are paid back to shareholders. Dividends are not guaranteed and may fluctuate from one reporting period to the next.

- Money market funds are considered low risk investments compared to other mutual funds.
- Investors are provided a prospectus or profile outline performance and annual reports.
- Most funds require a minimum initial investment (between $500 and $5,000).
- You may be allowed to write a limited number of checks against your account per month.
- Deposits are not guaranteed by FDIC/FSLIC insurance.
- Interest earned is taxable.
- There is no guarantee rate of return and interest earned may vary.
- Fees charged to participate in a money market fund are higher than a regular money market account.

Money Market Account (MMA)

- Interest is calculated on a fixed annual yield rate.
- Interest is taxable.
- A minimum balance may be required to open an account.
- There are withdrawal restrictions. You are limited to six transfers or withdrawals per month with no more than three transactions as checks written against the account.
- Deposits are guaranteed by FDIC/FSLIC insurance up to $100,000 per account.
- Your money is accessible any time (although there are restrictions)
- The interest rate paid by a financial institution on a money market account is usually higher than its CD or passbook savings rate.

The Solution

Although all savings vehicles are useful, where to place your money is directly tied to your immediate and long-term needs.

- If you need access to your money, a savings account or money market account may be a better choice for you.
- If you do not think you will need the money right away, put it in a CD where you may not be able to access it easily but you will earn a little higher interest.
- If you need access to your money but want it to earn a higher interest rate, a money market fund or account might be a better option.

Shop Around

Just as you do not do all your shopping at one store, you should not put all your money in one bank. Shop for the best CD, money market fund or savings interest rate. Banks, like stores, offer specials to attract new customers. You might get a better CD rate at one bank and a better money market rate at another.

Compare Costs

Because of possible fees, you should always shop around and compare what different banks are offering. Things you should look at include:

1. Fees and services charges on the account;
2. minimum balance requirements;
3. interest rate paid on your balance; and
4. management and early withdrawal penalties.

The Resources

www.imoneynet.com/

Informa Financial Company, has been collecting and reporting money fund statistics since 1975.

www.sec/gov/answers/mfmmkt.htm

The U.S. Securities and Exchange Commission Website contains information about money market funds.

www.ici.org/index/html

Investment Company Institute is the national association of U.S. investment companies and promotes public understanding of mutual funds and other investment companies.

http://beginnersinvest.about.com/cs/banking/a/062501a.htm

This Website contains articles on money market accounts, CDs and money market funds.

www.productresearch.info

This Website identifies industry leaders and provides a list of companies and possible resources that consumers can use as a product research tool. The site is updated every three hours.

http://money.howstuffworks.com/question724.htm

The how stuff works Website provides answers to thousands of questions on thousands of topics.

18
Bonds

The Challenge

Bonds are boring. There is nothing exciting about investing your money into a bond. But bonds can play an exciting role in the health of your retirement portfolio. As part of a well-managed portfolio, bonds can be a dependable source of steady, fixed income available for you to spend or re-invest.

A bond is a loan you make to the U.S. Government, a state, a local municipality or a company. Companies and governments need this money to finance projects like new buildings and roads. The corporation or government, over a stated period of time, pays you back the amount borrowed, plus interest. In essence, you are loaning the government or company your money.

Why would you want to invest in bonds? To balance your investment portfolio.

The Facts

Bonds are a steady investment that virtually guarantees a return over a longer period of time. To break it down into monetary terms: If you buy a $1,000 bond (in essence lend) with a payback period of 10 years at 9 percent interest, then the $1,000 is the face value (also known as the par value) of the bond; the yearly 9 percent interest payment is the coupon; and the length of the loan, 10 years, is the bond's maturity. At the end of 10 years you will have earned $900 in interest and will get your initial $1,000 investment back.

Bonds are often referred to as fixed-income securities. The interest earned from a bond is counted as income. When you purchase a bond, the bond issuer promises that you will receive the agreed upon interest and the full amount of your investment back. In comparison, if you purchase stock in a company, the issuing company does not promise a return of your initial investment, an increase in the value of the stock or even the prospect of a dividend. Bonds yield predictable returns over time and work to balance a portfolio. Bonds will never be part of a get rich quick scheme, yet there are several great reasons that they should be included in your portfolio.

There are different types of bonds. Most bonds are issued by one of three groups:

1. U.S. government or federal agencies.
2. State and local governments.
3. Corporations.

U.S. Government Bonds

The U.S. Government offers the safest kinds of bonds. Bonds issued by the U.S. government are often called treasuries because they are issued by the U.S. Treasury Department and are fully backed by the U.S. government. In exchange for a smaller degree of risk, investors will receive a lower interest rate than other comparable bonds from different issuers. There are four types of treasuries:

1. Bills–mature from 90 days to 1 year
2. Notes–mature from 2 to 10 years
3. Bonds–mature over 10 to 30 years
4. Savings bonds–redeemable without penalty after 5 years

You do not pay state or local taxes on any interest income you make on treasury bonds. Savings bonds can be bought in very small amounts and are designed for small investors.

Municipal Bonds

Bonds offered by state and local governments, or municipalities, are known as municipal bonds. Any interest income you make on a municipal bond is free from federal income taxes and from state and local income tax in some states.

Government Agency Bonds

Even though a bond is issued by a government agency it is not backed by the U.S. government, just by the agency that issued it–who carries only a moral obligation to pay the full amount agreed. The three best-known agencies are Freddie Mac, Ginnie Mae and Fannie Mae. These agencies offer mortgage-backed securities that provide higher yields than treasuries. The interest income of these types of bonds can fluctuate over the life of the bond.

Corporate Bonds

Corporate bonds attract a larger number of investors because they offer a higher yield than any other bond–up to two or more percentage points higher. Corporate bonds are considered riskier than treasuries and most municipal bonds because competition, economic conditions and even mismanagement can lead to uncertainty about a company's ability to pay bondholders and other creditors.

However, risk may have its rewards. The lower the company's credit quality, the higher the interest rate you will be offered for buying the bond.

Corporate bonds come in three maturity ranges:

- Short-term: 1 to 5 years
- Intermediate term: 5 to 15 years
- Long-term: 15 or more years

Other Types of Bonds

Zero-Coupon Bonds

This type of bond is issued with no coupon rate at all. The Treasury Department, corporations, municipalities and government agencies issue zero-coupon bonds. With a zero-coupon bond you purchase the bond at a deep discounted rate, meaning you purchase it for less than its face value. The difference between a zero-coupon bond and other bonds is you will not receive a steady payout stream over time. Upon maturity you will receive a lump sum payout of the principal and interest. Good reasons to invest in this type of bond is for your child's college tuition or if you wish to receive a lump sum amount upon retirement. You will pay taxes on the interest earned before you receive the payout, which may be an unexpected financial strain for some investors.

Junk Bonds

These are high-yield bonds with a higher degree of risk. The risk is that the issuing company may not earn enough money to cover the interest payments to investors every 6 months. Junk bonds come from companies who are less creditworthy and there is always a danger they may not repay the principal and interest during down economic times.

The Solution

Laddering

As every financial expert advises, the key to sound investing is diversification. The three main places to invest your money are stocks, bonds and cash. Keep in mind that interest rates and bond prices move in opposite directions. When interest rates go up, bond prices go down and vice versa. Building a balanced portfolio will keep your investment strategy steady.

A good bond investing strategy to offset interest rate ups and downs is called bond laddering. Laddering is a strategy that uses maturity weighting, which involves dividing your money among several bonds with staggered maturity dates. This investment strategy is often recommended to investors who are interested in using bonds to generate income. Laddering is used to minimize both interest rate risk and reinvestment risk.

Here is a look at how it works: If interest rates rise, you reinvest the bonds that are maturing at the bottom of your ladder into higher-yielding bonds. If rates fall, you are protected against reinvestment risk because you have longer-maturity bonds at the top of your ladder that are not affected by the drop in rates. For example, you buy a 2-year bond, a 4-year bond, and a 6-year bond. If you put equal amounts of money into each bond, the average maturity of the entire portfolio would be 4 years. As each bond matures, you would then replace it with a bond equal to the longest maturity in your portfolio. So if a 2-year bond matures, you replace with a 6-year bond. Your older bonds are now 2 years closer to maturity so the average weighted maturity of your portfolio remains the same—4 years.

Laddering provides you with better interest rate protection than if you owned bonds of a single maturity. If interest rates fall you may consider investing your bonds at the shortest maturity date at a lower interest rate, but your gain would be an above market return from the longer maturity rates. On the flip side, if rates go up your total bond investment will receive a below-market return, but you could make adjustments when your shorter-term bonds mature.

As with any investment, there are risks and one risk to laddering is that your return may be lower than a non-laddered bond portfolio.

The Resources

www.investingbonds.com

> The Bond Market Association provides a calculator to determine equivalent taxable yield on municipal bonds for you.

www.moneychimp.com

> This Website provides the bond yield to maturity formula.

www.ehow.com/how_16557_calculate-bonds-yields.html

> This Website shows you how to calculate bond yields to maturity.

19

Tax-Exempt &
Tax-Deferred Investments

The Challenge

Tax reduction should not be your primary objective when choosing an investment. You should try to preserve your investment by building a balanced portfolio, including investing in tax-exempt and tax-deferred programs. While they may sound alike there are differences:

- Tax-exempt means owing no taxes when the investment is sold or when you start taking distribution payments at age 59½.
- Tax-deferred means paying taxes on the investment when it is sold or when you start taking distribution payments at age 59½.

The distinction is small but can make a big difference in the amount of income you may keep each year tax-free and how much you must pay taxes on.

The Facts

Tax-Exempt

- Taxes are not owed on money you earn from the investment.
- The interest only from tax-free investments is exempt from federal taxes, and possibly state and local taxes. Capital gains, however, may still be taxed.
- Examples of a tax-free investment include municipal bonds and a Roth IRA (if withdrawals are made more than 5 years after the Roth IRA was established).
- Withdrawing your money before age 59½ will result in a penalty and your money will be taxed at possibly a higher rate.

Advantages

If you hold an investment for more than a year before you sell, you will owe tax on any increase in value at a long-term capital gains rate of 15 percent or 5 percent, depending on your tax bracket. However, if the investment becomes worth less than you paid for it, you can sell it, take the loss and use the amount lost to offset capital gains. You may deduct excess capital losses to offset up to $3,000 per year of ordinary income.

Tax-Deferred

- Taxes are not owed on the investment until it is sold.
- The interest from tax-deferred investments is paid when you sell the investment or begin taking distribution payments at age 59½.
- Examples of a tax-deferred investment include salary reduction plans such as 401(k), 403(b), Section 457 plans, SEPs and SIMPLEs.
- Withdrawing your money before age 59½ will result in a penalty and your money will be taxed at possibly a higher rate.

Advantages

A major advantage of tax-deferred investing is making contributions to a retirement plan with your pre-tax dollars. These contributions reduce your taxable income so you pay fewer taxes now, reducing the amount of taxes deducted from your paycheck and leaving you more to invest.

For example, if you are in the 35 percent income tax bracket and you contribute $1,000 to a tax-deferred retirement plan, you are lowering your federal income taxes by $350 (0.35 times $1,000).

A second advantage to tax-deferred savings plans is your earnings grow faster because they are not taxed until they are withdrawn. Instead of paying taxes on interest earned, the interest is reinvested into the fund and your money continues to compound until either the investment is sold or you begin taking contributions at age 59½. Over time, the gap between the value of a taxable and a tax-deferred account, earning the same rate of interest, increases sharply.

What is the difference you will pay in taxes on income earned between a tax-exempt and a tax-deferred investment? The tables below shows the difference.

Tax-Deferred	
Contributions	$5,000/year
Interest	5 percent
Tax bracket	28 percent
Contribution length	25 years
Taxed ending balance	$204,465
Tax-deferred ending balance	$250,567
Tax savings	$46,102

Tax-Exempt	
Contributions	$500/month
Interest	5 percent
Tax bracket	28 percent
Contribution length	25 years
After-tax retirement income	$3,472
Amount of income that is taxable	$2,973
Amount that is not taxable	$499
Tax savings spread over 20 years*	$119,760

*Based on monthly withdrawals from age 65 to 85.

The Solution

You can see from the comparison how much you will save on taxes on tax-deferred versus tax-exempt investments.

The next step is to compare a tax-exempt investment to a taxable investment. Tax-exempt investments will almost always produce a higher yield than a taxable investment. The question is by much more? To illustrate the differences between a tax-exempt and taxable investment, use this formula to figure out how much more you would have to earn on a taxable investment to equal your tax-exempt earnings.

Consider, for example you might earn 5 percent on a tax-exempt investment. If you were in the 28 percent tax bracket you would need to earn 6.94 percent on a taxable investment to achieve the same return.

$$\frac{\text{Tax-exempt yield}}{100 - \text{your tax rate}} \times 100 = \text{Equivalent taxable yield}$$

or

$$5 \div (100\text{-}28) \times 100 = 6.94\% \text{ taxable equivalent yield}$$

There are a number of other ways you can reduce your tax liability on your investments:

- Reduce your tax liability by adding tax-exempt municipal bonds in your overall plan. These bonds are issued by state or local governments, often to raise money for building or improvement projects or to pay for day-to-day operating expenses. The downside is municipal bonds generally pay less interest than taxable corporate or treasury bonds, but you are usually exempt from paying federal tax on your earnings, making them a relatively safe investment vehicle.
- Make sure the bonds are purchased in the state you currently reside in so the earnings are exempt from state tax.
- If you are in a higher tax bracket and the state in which you live has a high income tax rate, tax-exempt will save you from paying a large portion of your earnings to taxes.

- Consider investing through a Roth IRA. Contributions are made after-tax, but withdrawals are tax-free provided that you are at least 59½ when you take the money out and your account has been open at least 5 years.
- If you are investing to pay education expenses, consider investing in tax-free Coverdell Education Savings Accounts (ESAs) or 529 college savings plans. Be aware of the rules about how the money can be spent to qualify for tax-free treatment.

Most financial advisers agree that tax-exempt plans are better than tax-deferred plans. However, you should participate in any tax-deferred retirement plan that is available at your job, even if it is the only investing you are doing.

The type of investments you choose depends on your desired return and the tax consequences of that type of investment. While reducing your taxes and earning more is always preferable, balancing your portfolio may be your number one priority. Regardless, understanding the factors that will affect the outcome of your investment is paramount for smart planning.

The Resources

www.savecalc.com/?gclid=CJ6Aw8eoyYQCFSUySAodKEKHKg

Calculate how much your savings will be worth at your desired retirement age.

www.mostchoice.com/global/calculators/taxdefer0.cfm

MostChoice provides investment, mortgage and insurance calculators and quotes and assistance to locating independent local agents to investors.

www.pacificlife.com/Channel/Educational+Information/Calculators/ Power+of+Tax+Deferral.htm

Use this Website to access the power of tax-deferral by using the deferral calculator from Pacific Life Insurance.

Cash-Balance
Defined-Benefit Plans

The Challenge

Once upon a time if you were a loyal employee and worked for a company for 10 or more years you were rewarded for your service with a nice watch and generous pension check. Employer-sponsored retirement plans have changed considerably in recent years. Since the early 1980s, there has been a slow shift away from the traditional defined-benefit pension plan to the more employer friendly defined-contribution plan.

Here is a short distinction between the two plans:

- A defined-benefit plan is a fixed-rate interest plan that provides a specific benefit at retirement for each eligible employee. They are employer-funded and the employee becomes vested after 10 years. If the employee leaves the company before becoming vested, the employee loses the pension.
- A defined-contribution plan is a variable rate interest plan that provides a specific benefit for each eligible employee. The actual retirement benefit amount depends on the amount of the contribution and market performance.

In an effort to cut costs and risks, a new plan has evolved that combines the elements of the traditional defined-benefit plan with the flexibility of a 401(k) plan. This new plan is called a cash-balance defined-benefit plan. As companies slowly phase out more costly defined-benefit plans, the challenge employees face today is to understand how cash-balance contribution plans work, the benefits and the pitfalls and, most importantly, how cash-balance defined plans are calculated.

The Facts

Younger employees love cash-balance pension plans while older employees hate them. The reason why is younger employees benefit from a cash-balance plan while older employees may not. A cash-balance plan does not reward an employee's longevity and age with higher benefits like a defined-benefit plan. Also, defined-benefits increase in amount as you age and the percentage of contributions. However, a cash-balance plan offers more portability than traditional pension plans, making it attractive to younger workers who can take their vested account as a lump sum when they leave the company or roll it over into another qualified pension plan.

To be eligible to participate in the cash-balance plan, you only need to be an employee for 5 years, which is half the time you needed to work before becoming fully vested in a defined-benefits plan. The cash-balance plan considers just one thing—your salary. You, the employee, do not make contributions, and when you retire, you receive your money as a lump sum or an annuity. The advantages to a cash-balance plan are good for employees in their 20s, okay for those in their 30s and even less attractive for those in their 40s.

Unlike defined-benefit plans, cash-balance plans do not guarantee benefits. The money deposited into your fixed or variable interest rate account may produce small, steady growth or may produce higher or lower returns depending on market conditions.

These benefits are available in either a lump sum or an annuity at retirement.

There are four major differences between typical cash balance plans and 401(k) plans.

1. Participation:
   The typical cash-balance plans does not require the workers to contribute part of their compensation to the plan; however, participation in a 401(k) plan does depend, in whole or in part, on an employee choosing to make a contribution to the plan.
2. Investment risks:
   The employer shoulders the risks and rewards of the investments in a cash-balance plan whereas participants in a 401(k) plan direct their own investments and take the risks and rewards from their investment allocations.
3. Life annuities:
   Cash-balance plans offer employees the option of receiving their benefits in the form of a lifetime annuity payout.
4. Federal guarantee:
   Since they are defined-benefit plans, the benefits promised by cash-balance plans are usually insured by a federal agency, the Pension Benefit Guaranty Corporation (PBGC). Defined-contribution plans, such as 401(k) plans, are not insured by the PBGC.

The amount deposited into an employee's account is based on a formula of a fixed percentage of earnings and percentages that vary by age, service or earnings. Deposits are made into each employee's account in the form of benefit credits. The following chart explains the calculation of benefit credits based on service.

Annually, each employee receives a benefit credit for the preceding year. A benefit credit is a percentage of pay that is determined by years of service, as shown:

Years of service	Percentage of pay
Less than 5	2 %
5 to 9	4 %
10 to 14	6 %
15 to 19	8 %
20 and above	10 %

Under an age-plus-service plan, the percentage of pay is based on the sum of age plus service, as reflected in this example:

Age plus years of service	Percentage of pay
Less than 30	5%
30 to 39	6%
40 to 44	7%
45 to 49	8%
50 to 54	9%
55 to 59	10%
60 to 64	11%
65 to 69	12%
70 to 74	13%
75 to 79	14%
80 or more	15%

Interest accumulated throughout the year is usually deposited into the account at the end of the year.

Cash-balance plans, like 401(k) plans, must specify a normal retirement age and make benefits available in the form of an annuity. But unlike an annuity, the participant must be able to take the lump sum balance out of the plan at any time, regardless of the normal retirement age declaration. Workers who take such lump sums can maintain their pension benefit and avoid tax penalties by transferring funds into an IRA.

The Solution

When you become eligible to receive benefits under a cash-balance plan, the benefits that you receive are stated in terms of an account balance. For example, you have an account balance of $100,000 when you reach age 65. If you decide to retire at that time, you should have the right to an annuity of approximately $10,000 per year for life. In many cash-balance plans, however, you may instead choose to take a lump sum benefit equal to the $100,000 account balance.

If you are vested and choose to leave your employer for another job, you may elect to receive your accrued benefits in a lump sum, even if it is well before your full retirement age. That distribution can be rolled over into an individual retirement account (IRA) or to another plan if that plan accepts rollovers.

The benefits of a cash-balance plan are heavily dependent on your age.

- As a young employee, a cash-balance plan is a company perk you can take with you when you move to your next job.
- The long-time employee who is nearing retirement will witness a reduction in contributions from your employer. Under the cash-balance plan, the contribution you receive is a percentage of your salary, ranging from 4 percent to 8 percent (plus interest).
- The middle-aged employees are caught in the middle. Most would be better off taking the pension, if given a choice. But if you are earning very small raises and do not think you will stay with the company very long, the cash-balance plan could be a welcome change.

If you plan to make a switch from a defined-benefit plan to a cash-balance plan, be sure you factor in any other benefits when considering the impact of your pension conversion. It may be more beneficial to take a lump sum annuity payout and reinvest that money into a traditional or conduit IRA until you know what you want to do with the money.

The Resources

www.dol.gov/ebsa/FAQs/faq_consumer_cashbalanceplans.html

Information on cash-balance defined-benefit plans from the Department of Labor, Employee Benefit Security Administration.

www.pensionrights.org/pages/publications.html

Benefit plan publications by the Labor Department.

http://biz.yahoo.com/edu/edu_retire.html

For an article on the low-down on cash-balance benefit plans.

www.hot-to-retire.com

Unbiased information and skeletal strategies useful to senior citizens as well as young, successful individuals and families looking to retire early.

21

SEP-IRAs & the Small
Business Owner

The Challenge

This chapter is for small business owners or self-employed individuals. This chapter reviews the two different types of SEP accounts and how SEP accounts differ from other retirement vehicles.

As a small business owner, one of the most rewarding benefits you can offer to your employees, and yourself, is to set up a simplified employee pension (SEP) account. SEPs–aka SEP-IRAs–are specialized IRAs. A SEP plan provides the small business employer a simplified way to make contributions toward an employee's and his or her own retirement. As a small business owner, you set up an individual retirement account (IRA) for each employee (including yourself) and make contributions directly to each account. Contributions are based on the profitability of the business during the year. During a good year you can deposit the maximum amount, during mediocre years you can put in less, and if a year has been particularly bad, you can skip contributing altogether.

There are advantages to setting up a SEP program:

- SEP programs are simple and inexpensive to set up.
- SEPs are easy to administer, both internally and with the IRS.
- Contributions made to SEPs do not need to be filed with the IRS.
- SEPs do not commit you (the employer) to annual contributions.
- The plan may be terminated at any time.
- SEPs allow a self-employed person to contribute up to 13 percent of annual self-employment income, up to $44,000 in 2006, and up to 15 percent for employees.
- SEPs enable you to reduce your businesses tax liability each year while contributing to an employees retirement account at the same time.

The Facts

There are two types of SEP accounts, an employee plan and a self-employed plan.

To be eligible to participate in a SEP plan the employee must be:

- Twenty-one years or older;
- have worked for you in at least 3 of the last 5 years; and
- have received at least $450 (subject to annual cost-of-living adjustments) in compensation in 2006.

Other considerations:

- Contributions must be made in cash. You cannot contribute property. Compensation is defined by the Internal Revenue Code includes bonuses and overtime.
- Most SEPs require that allocations to all employees' SEP-IRAs be proportional to their salary/wages. If you are a self-employed owner, the contribution is based on net profit minus one-half self-employment tax minus the contribution for yourself.
- If an employee is older than 70½ years of age, you may still make contributions to his or her SEP. However, the participant must take the required minimum distributions each year.
- You can set up a SEP for your own business even if you participate in another employer's retirement plan.
- When determining maximum contribution amounts, you may only consider up to $220,000 of the employee's income (even if the income for the year is higher) and SEP contributions cannot exceed the lesser of 25 percent of compensation, or $44,000 for 2006. This amount is subject to annual cost-of-living adjustments for later years.
- If an eligible employee dies or quits working before the SEP contribution is made for the year, he or she must receive his or her share of the SEP contribution when it is made for the year.
- A SEP-IRA is treated the same as a traditional IRA and may be rolled over into a separate IRA but cannot be incorporated into an employer sponsored 401(k) plan.
- You may terminate the SEP at any time. You can stop funding these plans once they are terminated. To terminate a SEP plan you should notify your employees that the plan has been discontinued and notify the financial institution that you will no longer be making contributions and will terminate the contract or agreement with it. You do not need to notify the IRS of the plan's termination.

The Solution

You establish a SEP by adopting a SEP agreement with your eligible employees. There are three basic steps in setting up a SEP, all of which must be satisfied.

1. You must execute a formal written agreement. You can satisfy this written

agreement by adopting an Internal Revenue Service (IRS) model SEP using *Form 5305-SEP, Simplified Employee Pension–Individual Retirement Accounts Contribution Agreement*. You may also use a prototype SEP that was approved by the IRS. Approved prototype SEPs are offered by banks, insurance companies and other qualified financial institutions, or you may adopt an individually designed SEP.

2. You must give each eligible employee certain information about the SEP. If you establish the SEP using the *Form 5305-SEP*, any information you provide to participants must include a copy of the *Form 5305-SEP*, its instructions, and the other information listed in the *Form 5305-SEP* instructions. If you use a prototype SEP or individually designed SEP, you must provide similar information. Note: This form is not filed with the IRS, but is kept with your records.

3. A SEP-IRA must be set up for each eligible employee. SEP-IRAs can be set up with banks, insurance companies or other qualified financial institutions. The SEP-IRA is owned and controlled by the employee and you send the SEP contributions to the financial institution where the SEP-IRA is maintained. Even if the employee declines to participate in the program, you still must set up an account in their name.

SEP-IRAs are flexible. You do not have to contribute to it every year. However, because a SEP is a qualified plan, the amount you contribute each year for yourself and your employees must be equal and can be deducted from your earnings. The contributions are tax-deductible. In poor earning years you can skip contributing, and in good years you can put away the maximum.

If you set up a SEP account for your employees and yourself, you have to give your employees the same kind of SEP benefits you give yourself. If you contribute 10 percent of your earnings to your SEP, you have to contribute 10 percent of their earnings to accounts in their names.

When you set up a SEP account is also important. Since most self employed individuals, at the start of the year, cannot predict how profitable the business will be by the end of the year, most business owners wait until the end of the year to fund SEP accounts. It is a good idea to wait until the end of the tax year to make a contribution, especially since there are penalties for investing too much.

Figuring the amount you can contribute to a SEP is derived from a formula based on each individual's salary. Example: If an employee earned $25,000 in 2005, the maximum contribution you can make to his or her SEP-IRA is $6,250 (.25 x $25,000).

You can only consider the portion of the employee's compensation of $220,000 or less when figuring your compensation limit for that employee. However, $44,000 (20 percent) is the maximum contribution for an eligible employee.

Distributions are subject to IRA rules. You cannot prohibit distributions from a SEP-IRA and you cannot make your contributions on the condition that any part of them must be kept in the account. The penalties for early withdrawal remain the same as with the traditional IRA. Contributions are deductible. If you end the plan, you can rollover the account into an IRA without penalty to keep earning money on a tax-deferred basis.

The Resources

www.irs.gov/pub/irs-pdf/p560.pdf

Publication 560 *Retirement Plans for Small Businesses*.

www.investopedia.com/university/retirementplans/sepira/

Investopedia provides a tutorial on SEPs.

http://personal.fidelity.com/products/retirement/getstart/newacc/ sepiracalc.shtml.cvsr.

Fidelity provides a SEP-IRA contribution calculator.

22

When to Dump an Investment Dog

The Challenge

Financial planners will tell you that if your portfolio is properly diversified you will not have to worry about a bad investment (sometimes affectionally referred to as an investment dog). It is natural for your investments to coincide with a robust or slowing economy. If you have a balanced portfolio it is likely that some investments will generate a better return while others may fall below expectations. If your portfolio is out of balance your overall returns will be lower.

How do you know how your investments are really doing? Most investors think their investments are doing okay until they take time to do the math and find out the return on investment (sans deposits and returns) is poor, thus making it an investment dog.

One way to determine if your investments are doing well is to conduct a semi-annual or annual comparative analysis. If you are a novice stock investor you may find it difficult to figure out your actual return rate, as large balances and deposits can influence the overall performance of your portfolio. For example, if you make very large deposits throughout the year, your year-end balance might lead you to believe your investments have grown, when they may actually have been stagnant. Similarly, if you take out more money than you deposited throughout the year, your year-end balance may lead you to believe that investment growth was slow, when in fact it was robust.

This chapter is for the confident investor who invests primarily in stocks, although the formulas provided are also beneficial to the IRA investor who may learn he or she has a portfolio that needs balancing. You will learn how to calculate your actual returns and when it might be time to dump that investment dog.

The Facts

You can use the equation below to find out how your investments fared the past year.

$$\frac{\text{Year end balance - Start of year balance - Deposits + Withdrawals}}{\text{Start of year balance + (0.5 x Deposits)}-\text{(0.5 x Withdrawals)}}$$

Putting numbers to the formula will make it easier to understand.

Year end balance = $120,000
Start of year balance = $105,000
Deposits = $10,000
Withdrawals = $5,000

In numeric terms the formula will look like this:

$$\frac{\$120,000 - \$105,000 - \$10,000 + \$5,000}{\$105,000 + \$5,000 - \$2,500} = \frac{(\$\ 10,000)}{(\$107,500)}$$

Thus, $10,000/$107,500 equals .093 or a 9.3 percent return for the previous year.

The formula also works if the amount of withdrawals is larger the total amount of deposits.

$$\frac{\$120,000 - \$105,000 - \$10,000 + \$15,000}{\$105,000 + \$5,000 - \$7,500} = \frac{(\$\ 20,000)}{(\$102,500)}$$

Thus, $20,000/$102,500 equals .195 or a 19.5 percent return for the previous year.

The formula also works if the year-end balance is lower than the start balance.

$$\frac{\$105,000 - \$120,000 - \$10,000 + \$5,000}{\$120,000 + \$5,000 - \$2,500} = \frac{(-\$20,000)}{(\$122,500)}$$

Thus, negative $20,000 divided by $122,500 equals negative .0163 or a negative 1.63 percent return for the previous year.

This calculation works best for single investments or a group of securities and is only reliable as a single year calculation. It will not produce accurate results if you lump together a couple of year's worth of start balances, deposits or withdrawals. Each year must be calculated separately to give the most accurate results. The same principals apply to the type of investment you want to review. Each investment will generate different results, so calculate each investment separately (such as individual stocks) rather than in a group to learn which stock or investment is underperforming and should be dumped.

The Solution

It is important for a successful investor to analyze the results of each investment fully on an annual basis. If your investments as a sum are not meeting your required return on investment you should review each investment individually to determine which one is not performing and then take steps to change your portfolio to better producers.

Equally important as analyzing the real return rate is to plan an exit strategy (dumping the dog). Every investment should be purchased with an exit strategy in mind. Your exit strategy is a determination of when you should sell a stock or move money from one investment to another. If your financial plan requires a particular return on investment but an investment in your portfolio is not performing up to expectations, consider dumping it for another investment that will meet your expectations. The same theory applies to an investment that does not meet your return expectations more than 2 years in a row.

This is particularly important for any investor who invests then does not track the progress of the investment until it is too late or it has lost a significant amount of value. Many investors put money into investments that are showing a good return but fail to review the returns the following years only to realize the stock they bought at $70 a share is now worth $26 a share.

A common mistake many investors make is falling in love with their investments and holding on to a poor performer too long. Calculating your return rate for each investment on an annual basis takes away the subjectivity as to which investments to keep and which to dump. It is all there in black and white (or red if it is a loser). There, the decision has been made for you!

Here are some ways to minimize the number of investment dogs you may have in your portfolio:

- Review your rate of return for each investment at least once or twice a year–select a date and stick to it every year.
- Develop goals and exit strategies for each investment.
- Avoid putting large portions of your portfolio into a single investment or industry.
- Resist following the crowd. If everyone is buying into variable annuities or some other trendy investment, watch out–the high may soon be a low.
- Know when to dump an investment. If the returns begin to drop, it may be time to dump it.

Actively monitoring your investments will help you manage your portfolio for high returns. If your plan is outperforming your expectations, you do not need to make any adjustments. However, if you plan is underperforming, try to identify which investment is dragging your portfolio down and make changes.

The Resources

www.dogsofthedow.com.

This Website includes techniques for selecting high dividend stocks, the study of their past performance, a gauge of their current performance, and methods to get more out of dog investments.

www.betterinvesting.org/

Better Investing members are provided with a program of investment education and support for becoming successful lifetime investors.

www.fool.com.

Individual investors are educated, enriched and amused by the multimedia financial education company Motley Food at *www.fool.com.*

Virtual Banking

The Challenge

If you do not mind giving up the trip to the teller window or the quick chat with your friendly account manager, a virtual, e-bank or online bank will save you very real money. Virtual banks are simply banks without bricks. From a customer's perspective, they exist entirely on the Internet, where they offer much the same types of services as a brick and mortar institution and they follow all the same federal regulations. The benefit to the consumer is virtual banks pass the money they save on overhead, such as buildings and tellers, along to you in the form of higher yields, lower fees and more generous account thresholds.

Virtual banks, like traditional banks, offer a variety of expanded services, from basic checking and savings accounts to money markets, 401(k) retirement accounts, loans and even insurance. Although online banking has been around since 1995, the banking industry has been challenged with attracting new customers to a completely online system. Online banking is more safe and secure than ever, and customers are finally beginning to feel comfortable with the process. Virtual banks must follow many of the same laws and regulations of traditional banks. With so many online banking options, the challenge is to find an online bank that is insured and reputable and that will give you the best return on your investments.

The Facts

Opening an account at a virtual bank is easy and can be coordinated from almost anywhere by anyone who has a personal computer and an Internet connection. There is no need to transfer banks or close out existing accounts. In fact, most online banks require you to have a personal checking or savings account with a traditional banking institution so you can link your personal checking account to your online account. This way funds between accounts may be transferred without charge.

Account statements are generated monthly but can be viewed online at anytime. Your accounts may be linked to any number of accounts and each account may be linked to an ATM card.

The advantages to online banking include:

- Convenience. Virtual banks are always open. They are available 24 hours a day, 7 days a week with only a mouse click away.
- Seamlessness. No matter where you are, if a money problem arises you can easily log on to your online bank account and take care of business at any time. No more waiting in line to visit a teller or waiting for the bank to open in the morning. If you are an international traveler, you no longer need to place a call to the bank at 3:00 a.m.
- High speed. Transactions are executed and confirmed faster than traditional banks.
- Access. Manage all of your accounts, including IRAs, CDs and even securities from one secure site. Your money is available anytime.
- Effectiveness. Most online banking sites now offer sophisticated tools and services, including account aggregation, stock quotes, rate alerts and portfolio managing programs to help you manage all of your assets more effectively. Most are also compatible with money managing programs such as Quicken and Microsoft Money.
- Security. Recent studies have shown that online banking customers were less likely to fall victim to identity theft than account holders at traditional paper banks.

The disadvantages of online banking include:

- A longer start-up time. In order to register for your bank's online program, you will probably have to provide ID and sign a form at a bank branch. If you and your spouse wish to view and manage your assets together online, one of you may have to sign a durable power of attorney before the bank will display all of your holdings together.
- A learning curve. Plan to invest some time and/or read the tutorials in order to become comfortable in your virtual lobby.
- Technological changes. Periodic changes to online programs may require you to re-enter account information with each upgrade.
- Building trust. For many people, the biggest hurdle to online banking is learning to trust it. Banks are beginning to build safeguards into programs to eliminate confusion.
- ATM inaccessibility. Because most virtual banks do not have ATM machines, they will typically charge the same user fee that your brick-and-mortar bank would if you used another bank's ATM. Plus, many virtual banks do not accept deposits via ATM; you will have to either deposit the check by mail or transfer money from another account.

The Solution

Despite some disadvantages, virtual banking can save you money on fees and charges and yield you a better return on your investments. While a difference in interest of 1 percent may not seem like much, the total interest earned over the life of the investment may be substantial. Most online banks offer CDs and 401(k) funds at a full percentage point higher than traditional banks. As with investing money at any financial institution, there are ways you can safeguard your money. Before opening an account with an online bank, research the bank thoroughly.

- Confirm that the online bank is legitimate and that your deposits are fully insured by the Federal Deposit Insurance Corporation (FDIC). The FDIC warns consumers that not all banks operating on the Internet are insured by the FDIC. Many banks that are not FDIC-insured are chartered overseas. Check with your bank or the FDIC if you are not certain.
- Keep your personal information private and secure. Phishing scams are often cleverly disguised as legitimate communications from your bank. Most online banks make it a practice to never request sensitive personal information via email. If you receive an email asking for social security, password or account information contact your online bank immediately to verify its authenticity.
- Understand your rights as a consumer. Online bank customers are guaranteed the same rights as traditional brick and mortar customers.
- Learn where to go for more assistance from banking regulators. Also, you should check the FDIC's online database of FDIC-insured institutions. You can search by name, city, state or zip code of the bank, and click the Find button. A positive match will display the official name of the bank, the date it became insured, its insurance certificate number, the main office location for the bank (and branches), its primary government regulator, and other links to detailed information about the bank. If your bank does not appear on this list, contact the FDIC.
- Most bank Websites have an About Us section or something similar that describes the institution. You may find a brief history of the bank, the official name and address of the bank's headquarters, and information about its insurance coverage from the FDIC. To verify a bank's insurance status, look for the familiar FDIC logo or the words Member FDIC or FDIC Insured on the Website.
- Protect yourself from fraudulent Websites. For example, watch out for copycat Websites that deliberately use a name or web address very similar to, but not the same as, that of a real financial institution. The intent is to lure you into clicking onto their Website and giving your personal information, such as your account number and password. Always check to

see that you have typed the correct Website address for your bank before conducting a transaction and make sure the URL listed is accurate.

- It is important to safeguard your banking information, credit card numbers, Social Security Number and other personal data. Look at your bank's Website for information about its security practices, or contact the bank directly.

    –The virtual bank should have encryption features that scramble private information to prevent unauthorized access. Avoid sending sensitive information, such as account numbers, through unsecured e-mail.

    –You should use a passwords or personal identification number (PIN) when accessing your account online. Your password should be unique to you and you should change it regularly. Do not use birthdates or other numbers or words that may be easy for others to guess.

    –Remember to update your personal computer virus protection frequently.

    –If you click on non-financial Websites that are linked to your bank's site, be aware that they are not FDIC insured.

The Resources

To view some online banks

www.bankofinternet.com, and
https//www.oneunited.com/ (First black-owned Internet bank).

The Federal Deposit Insurance Corporation has many Website pages to assist you with online banking.

www2.fdic.gov/starsmail

Customer assistance form where you can ask a question or make a complaint;

www.fdic.gov/consumers/questions/index.html

FDIC Consumer assistance.

www2.fdic.gov/edie

A calculator to determine your insurance coverage at FDIC-Insured banks.

www.fdic.gov/deposit/deposits/insured/index.html

General information about the Federal Deposit Insurance Corporation.

www.fdic.gov/consumers/consumer/rights/index.html

Information about consumer financial rights.

24

What Credit Unions
Have to Offer

The Challenge

Credit unions originated in Europe in the mid-1800s. The first credit union in the United States was formed in Manchester, New Hampshire in 1909. Today, more than 10,000 credit unions with over $480 billion in assets serve more than 79 million people in the United States. According to the American Banker Newspaper's annual customer satisfaction survey, credit unions have been rated No. 1 in customer satisfaction at financial institutions for the past 10 years.

A credit union is a non-profit, cooperative financial institution owned and run by its members. Organized to serve, democratically controlled credit unions provide members with a safe place to save and borrow at reasonable rates. Members pool their funds in a co-operative fashion to make loans to one another. A volunteer board is elected by the members to run the organization.

How does a chapter on credit unions relate to retirement planning? As a retiree your goal is to preserve as much income as you can. Credit unions offer lower rates to their customers. Becoming a member of a credit union may be beneficial to your retirement planning. You may realize a greater return on your investments and your retirement dollars may stretch further at a credit union.

The Facts

What makes a credit union different from other financial institutions is that thrifts, banks and savings & loans (S&Ls) are owned by groups of stockholders whose main objective is to earn healthy returns on their investments. Credit unions are operated as non-profits and the operating principles have remained unchanged: (1) only people who are credit union members should borrow there; (2) loans are made for prudent and productive purposes; (3) a person's desire to repay (character) is considered more important than the ability (income) to repay. Members are, after all, borrowing their own money and that of their friends. These principles still govern most of the world's credit unions.

Unlike a bank, which has stockholders, a credit union's members are its shareholders, and each member has an equal say (one vote) in the governance of the credit union. Earnings from the credit union are reinvested back to member shareholders in the form of lower fees, higher dividends, better rates and more services.

Credit unions are available for everyone, but the law places some limits on the people they may serve. A credit union's charter defines its field of membership. Most credit unions are organized to serve people in a particular community, group or groups of employees, or members of an organization or association. To join a credit union, you must be eligible for membership as each institution decides whom it will serve.

Credit unions are known for their strong financial condition. Credit unions, like other financial institutions, are closely regulated. The National Credit Union Share Insurance Fund (NCUSIF), administered by the National Credit Union Adminstration, an agency of the federal government, insures deposits of credit union members at more than 9,000 federal and state-chartered credit unions nationwide. Like banks and S&Ls, credit unions are highly regulated financial institutions, and their members' deposits enjoy identical protection to FDIC coverage up to $100,000 per customer (individual or business) and $250,000 per retirement account under the National Credit Union Share Insurance Fund. Credit unions also have the distinction of not costing the American taxpayer a penny in bailouts. By contrast, the S&L failures in the 1980s and 1990s cost taxpayers approximately $124 billion. The General Accounting Office, after completing a comprehensive study of credit unions in 2003, found that credit unions have a greater proportion of assets available to cover potential losses than banks and thrifts.

Credit union membership continues to increase steadily. Capital ratios, representing a credit union's net worth, are at their highest levels ever, while loan delinquency rates continue to drop. The National Credit Union Share Insurance Fund, the federal fund that insures credit union deposits, continues to be the strongest deposit insurance fund in the nation. The average size of a credit union is $65 million, while the average size of bank is nearly $1 billion. Over half of credit unions have less than $10 million in assets.

Historically, credit unions offered only savings accounts and consumer loans. Many of the larger credit unions have responded to their members' changing–and more sophisticated–financial needs. Some credit unions offer credit cards, debit cards, checking accounts, IRAs and share certificates. Credit unions also are expanding the types of loans they offer. Many offer mortgages, home equity loans, student loans and small business loans to members.

The Solution

With no investor presence, credit unions are able to pass the big savings directly to each member through lower rates on loans and mortgages than banks, and higher interest returns on deposit accounts. Larger credit unions now offer a wide variety of products to members, including insurance services such as dental, long-term care, business, mortgage, life, auto, home and rental, as well as credit cards, retirement planning, and more, making the benefits of membership even more attractive.

By concentrating on serving a defined group of people, credit unions are able to concentrate on the needs of their members to provide a personalized level of service and dedication to the communities where they do business.

To locate a credit union in your area:

- Call your state league to find out about unions in your area that you may be eligible to join. You can also visit *www.ncua.gov/indexdata.html* to locate a credit union in your state.
- Talk with your boss and co-workers. Your company may sponsor a credit union or may be a Select Employee Group (SEG) that has access to a credit union. Many employers offer direct deposit of payroll to credit unions.
- Poll your family. Does your spouse's employer sponsor a credit union? Most credit unions allow credit union members' families to join. Each credit union, however, may define who is an eligible family member differently. At some, only members of your immediate family are eligible. At others, family may include extended family members, such as cousins, uncles and aunts.
- Ask the neighbors. Some credit unions have a community field of membership, serving a region defined by geography rather than by employment or some other association. Ask friends in the community if they know of a credit union you may join.
- Search the yellow pages or utilize online search engines. Most credit unions rarely advertise, so you might not know about them unless you look them up.
- Contact The Credit Union National Association to help you find a credit union by calling 800.358.5710.
- Check the CUNA online database of credit unions at *www.cuna.org*.

The Resources

www.creditUnion.coop

For more information on credit unions.

www.nafcu.org

The National Association of Federal Credit Unions.

www.cuna.org

The Credit Union National Association.

www.ncua.gov

The National Credit Union Association.

25

Your Credit Score &
How to Boost It

The Challenge

Nothing can hurt you more financially than having bad credit. When you fill out an application for credit from a bank, store or credit card company that information is forwarded to the credit bureaus along with constant updates on the status of your account. Your credit information is then calculated into your credit rating score (previously called your FICO score). Your credit score is a guideline used by lenders to measure your credit worthiness–a prediction of sorts of how you will repay your debts.

Recently the three top credit reporting agencies–Equifax, Experian and TransUnion–announced that they are introducing a new scoring system called VantageScore. The new scores are based on a single formula designed to make it easier for financial institutions to evaluate loan applications. This new scoring tool will be unveiled to consumers in the latter half of 2006.

Until recently, a credit score was known as FICO (named after the company Fair Isaacs Corporation who developed it). The score determined an individual's creditworthiness. The original FICO scores ranged between 350 and 850. The higher your number the less risk you represent to lenders and the better credit terms you will be extended by the lender.

A poor credit rating will cost you thousands of dollars in higher interest rates. The higher rates will reduce the amount of money you can save towards retirement. Your challenge is to demystify the elements that make up your credit rating, review your credit report for inaccuracies and increase your credit rating.

The Facts

The new credit rating system, VantageScore, will use a single formula and will create the scores for all three credit bureaus. The new system will no longer use numbers to rate customers; instead, a letter grading system will be implemented.

A = Excellent (901-990)
B = Good (801-900)
C = Average (701-800)
D = Risky (601-700)
F = Too Risky (501-600)

An A or B credit grading means your interest rate on a home loan will probably be four percentage points lower than someone who has a C or D grade. To put it in financial terms, over the life of a 30-year mortgage, you will pay $200,000 less in interest.

It seems everyone is using your credit report rating to evaluate you as a worthy person. Some employers will review every job applicant's credit score for financial problems, such as poor credit history and bankruptcy, and may make a job offer contingent on a good credit rating. Insurance companies, banks, credit card companies and landlords are all peeking at your scores.

Bringing up your credit score to the highest level possible and keeping it there will increase your ability to earn and save more money for retirement.

While the exact mathematical formula for determining a credit score is a closely guarded secret, your score is created using a formula similar to this:

35% - Your Payment History

This includes the number of accounts paid as agreed, delinquent accounts and collection attempts. Delinquent accounts measure the total number of past due items, how long they have been past due and how long since you had a past due payment.

30% - Amounts You Owe

The amounts you owe includes how much you owe on accounts and the types of accounts with balances, how much of your revolving credit you have used the amounts you owe on installment loan accounts versus the original loan amount (to make sure you are paying the loans down) and the number of zero balance accounts.

15% - Length of Your Credit History

This includes how long you have had credit, the length of time since the accounts were opened and the amount of time since the last activity on the accounts.

10% - Types of Credit Used

Types of credit used refers to the total number of accounts and types of accounts (installment, revolving, mortgage). A mixture of account types will produce a better score than reports with only revolving credit accounts.

10% - New Credit

New credit is the number of accounts you have recently opened and the number of recent credit inquiries.

Who has a good credit score?

A look at credit scores among the US population in 2003 reveals:

Credit Score	Percentage of the population
Up to 499:	1%
500 - 549:	5%
550 - 599:	7%
600 - 649:	11%
650 - 699:	16%
700 - 749:	20%
750 - 799:	29%
Over 800:	11%

Amazingly, most people do not take the time to review their credit history and are not aware it could contain erroneous or outdated information. It is to every consumer's advantage to review his or her credit history with all three bureaus at least once a year to make sure the information is accurate. False or old information on your report is costing you money and could be hurting your chances to increase your earnings.

The Solution

Some lenders review the scores from all three reports, while others might look at only one. Mortgage lenders usually look at all three and make decisions based on the middle grade.

It is important to note that you do no lose any credit points for checking your own credit report, but you will lose some points if your report contains a number of credit inquiries over time for applications such as credit cards, auto loans, department store credit cards, etc. Each time you apply for credit, a credit inquiry is initiated, which in turn can lower your credit score by as much as five points. The next time you are offered a 10 percent off your purchase today by signing up with a store credit card, keep in mind that you may be saving a few dollars now but it may be quietly lowering your credit score.

If you are shopping for a big ticket item, like a car or mortgage, credit inquiries are inevitable. However, if you keep all the inquiries to a 2-week period, credit scoring companies will treat all the inquiries as one.

A law enacted in 2003 allows you to review your history and credit score from each of the credit bureaus once a year for free. Request a copy of your credit score to make sure everything on your credit report is correct. If you see something wrong, you can file a dispute with the agency in writing, online or by email. Never file a dispute by phone. It is better to keep a written record as proof the information has been corrected. By law, the creditor must prove the accuracy of what you are disputing within 30 days. If they do not, it gets removed from your report.

If you have evidence that something is wrong, then submit the evidence via a registered delivery service to the credit agency and they will have to remove the inaccurate data right away or prove that it is accurate. If disputing these items has not worked, you will have to contact the creditor or collection agency directly.

A low credit score will result in additional points on a mortgage or a higher interest rate or the real possibility you will not qualify for credit at all. It is never too late to start building good credit. A good credit rating creates countless opportunities.

The Resources

www.CreditBureauReportsOnline.com

Check your creditworthiness with a free credit report in seconds.

www.myfico.com

FICO credit scores, online credit reports and identity theft protection.

To obtain your free credit report score from:

Equifax	www.equifax.com	800.685.1111
Experian	www.experian.com	888.397.3742
TransUnion	www.annualcreditreport.com	800.888.4213

26

The Right Credit Card for You

The Challenge

A little short on cash this week? Not a problem, the mail will be arriving soon with a new round of credit card offers. Every day credit card companies send millions of invitations to consumers to apply for their credit card. *You are pre-approved for a $25,000 credit limit! Your Pre-approval is guaranteed!* These offers sound very exciting, especially to someone who may be cash strapped, a college student or just starting a career. It is easy money...too easy.

There is no universal credit card standard—each card issuer offers a different set of terms. Before you accept a card, shop around to get the best deal and ask a lot of questions. You want to find a card with features that match your needs best.

The Facts

How do you plan to use the credit card? If you pay your bill in full each month, then the grace period, rather than the annual fee, may be more important than the low periodic rate. If you plan to use the cash advance feature, be aware that many cards do not permit a grace period for the amounts due even if they have a grace period for purchases. If you plan to utilize the revolving credit option and carry a balance, the APR and finance charges will be important considerations. To help you find the right card and terms, review these facts.

The Annual Percentage Rate (APR) is one type of interest rate you will pay if you carry over a balance, withdraw a cash advance or transfer a balance to or from another card. The APR states the interest rate as a yearly rate. A single credit card may have multiple APRs.

- Fixed-Rate APRs remains constant until you receive written notification from the credit card company of a rate increase.
- Variable Rate APRs changes over time. The rate is often tied to another interest rate such as the Federal prime rate or the Treasury bill rate.
- Cash advance and Balance Transfer Rate APRs are often higher than the APR charged for regular purchases. For example, a 14 percent rate may

be charged for regular purchases, 19.9 percent for cash advances and 21 percent for balance transfers. Cash advance fees may not include a single digit percentage, but a flat rate fee plus a higher interest rate is applied to the advance. Be mindful that the fees can add up quickly.

- Tiered APRs are applied to different levels of the outstanding balance. For example, 16 percent on balances of $1 to $500 and 17 percent on balances above $500.
- Penalty Rate. The APR may increase if you are late making payments to your card issuer or any other card issuers. For example, if you pay any lender one day past the statement due date even once within a six-month period, an increase in your APR will take effect.
- A Delayed or Introductory Rate starts low for 6 months then jumps to the current APR.

Finance charges vary by lender. The finance charge is the dollar amount you pay for the privilege of credit being extended to you. The amount depends on your outstanding balance and the APR charged. To calculate the outstanding balance, credit card companies use one of several methods:

- Over one billing cycle or two;
- using the adjusted balance, the average daily balance, or the previous balance; and
- including or excluding new purchases in the balance.

Depending on the balance you carry and the timing of your purchases and payments, you will have a lower finance charge with one-cycle billing and either:

- The average daily balance method excluding new purchases;
- the adjusted balance method; or
- the previous balance method.

Some credit cards have a minimum finance charge. The minimum finance charge applies only when you carry a balance from one billing cycle to the next. Examples of the varying balance computation methods include the following:

Average Daily Balance
> This is the most common calculation. The card issuer tallies the beginning balance for each day in the billing period and subtracts any credits made to your account that day. The total is then divided by the number of days in the billing period.

Adjusted Balance
> This is the most advantageous method for cardholders. The adjusted balance is determined by subtracting payments or credits received during the current billing period from the balance at the end of the previous billing period. Purchases made during the current billing period are not included.

Previous Balance
> Reported as the amount you owed at the end of the previous
> billing period.

Two-cycle Balances
> An issuer calculates your finance charge by adding together your last two
> month's account activity.

The Grace Period, also referred to as a Free Period, is the number of days you
have to pay your bill in full before you start being charged interest. A grace period
is generally 25 days and applies only to new purchases–not for cash advances and
balance transfers. If your card includes a grace period, the issuer is required to
mail your bill a minimum of 14 days before the due date.

Credit card companies offer several different types of cards to fit any lifestyle:

- Secured cards are usually offered to people who have limited credit
  records, are just starting out or have had past credit troubles. Secured
  cards require the applicant to put up a security deposit to cover future
  purchases. The larger the security deposit, the higher your credit limit.
- Regular cards do not require a security deposit. Most regular cards have
  higher credit limits than secured cards but do not offer many incentives
  or perks.
- Premium cards (gold, platinum, titanium) offer higher credit limits,
  lower interest rates and extra features such as product warranties, travel
  insurance or emergency services.
- Affinity cards are all-purpose credit cards sponsored by professional
  organizations, college alumni associations or trade associations.
- Cash Back cards round up each purchase to the nearest dollar and
  deposit the change into a high yield savings account. Interest is calculated
  on the entire charge, so if you are not paying off your balance each
  month you are being charged a finance charge on the amount depostited
  into your savings account.

Review fee schedules carefully.

Annual fee.
> The annual fee is the amount charged yearly for the privilege to use
> the card.

Balance-transfer fee.
> This fee is charged when you transfer a balance from one credit card to
> another. If you plan on transferring balances from one card to another to
> take advantage of the lower rate, read the fine print very carefully. To lure
> you to try their card, some companies offer free balance transfers and
> lower interest rates.

Late-payment fee.
> This is the fee charged if your payment is received after the due date.

Over-the-credit-limit fee.

> If you request an increase in your credit limit, you may be charged an additional fee.

Set-up fee.

> May be disguised as an application fee when you open a new account.

Return-item fee.

> If your check bounces, you will be charged a non-sufficient funds or overdraft fee by both your bank and your card issuer.

Phone payment fees.

> You may incur a fee if you pay your bill by telephone or to cover the costs of reporting to credit bureaus, reviewing your account or providing other customer services.

The Solution

With so many different types of credit cards, you need to research each card's terms carefully before selecting a card that is right for you. How will you use your credit card? Keep these tips in mind when shopping for a credit or charge card:

- Shop around for the plan that best fits your needs.
- Make sure you understand a plan's terms before you accept the card.
- Hold on to receipts to reconcile charges when your bill arrives.
- Protect your cards and account numbers to prevent unauthorized use. Draw a line through blank spaces on charge slips so the amount cannot be changed. Tear up carbons.
- Keep a record of your cards in a safe place.
- Take the list of phone numbers, not the account numbers, with you when you travel, just in case a card is lost or stolen.
- Carry only the cards you think you will use.

Finally, review your statements carefully each month. Maintaining good credit will keep your interest rates low and your payments reasonable.

The Resources

www.creditcards.com

> Complete resource center that provides recent credit card articles. You can also search by type of card, bank or issuer and compare credit card offers.

www.bankrate.com

> Track and compare credit card rates and find out how much you can afford to owe.

www.federalreserve.gov/pubs/shop/survey.htm

> The Federal Reserve System provides a report that includes information from the largest credit card issuers in the country and other financial institutions.

27

What Is APR & How Does It Affect You?

The Challenge

The annual percentage rate (APR) can be an elusive number. Ask any mortgage banker or broker what makes up an APR and they will tell you that it depends on who you ask as the number may vary from lender to lender. The purpose of the APR is to prevent lenders from advertising a low rate and hiding fees. Yet, oddly enough, the APR was originally designed to measure the true cost of a loan and is supposed to create a level playing field for lenders and consumers.

The Federal Truth-in-Lending law requires mortgage companies to disclose the APR when they advertise a rate. Typically the APR acronym is found next to the rate like this:

6% APR

It does NOT affect your monthly payments. Your monthly payments are a function of the interest rate and the length of the loan.

The APR is the calculated amount of interest you pay on money that was advanced to you by a lending institution. In other words, on money that you borrow. Whether through a credit card purchase at a retail establishment for 10 or a one million dollar real estate transaction, how your rate or APR is calculated will affect how much interest you will pay on the loan.

When shopping for a favorable interest rate you should be able to compare APRs from lenders you are working with and pick the lowest rate. Simple right? Actually, it is not that simple. Most consumers are not aware that each lender can and does calculate their APRs differently! So it is buyer beware! A loan with a lower APR may not necessarily be a better rate. The reason why APRs are so difficult to compare is that the rules to compute APR are not clearly defined. Lenders may include some fees in the APR equation, but there is no standardization of what is included between lenders, leaving the consumer to wonder why two lenders with the same interest rate will have different monthly repayment amounts.

Squeezing every dollar from your current budget will be one more dollar towards financial success. Knowing how to compare what fees are included in the APR will help you get the best rate.

The Facts

What is APR?

APR is the cost of credit as a yearly rate. The percentage is derived from an equation that takes into account the total amount financed, finance charges and the term of the loan. The rate is calculated by taking the average compound interest rate over the term of the loan, enabling borrowers to compare loans. It is simply the periodic rate of interest multiplied by the number of periods in the year. For example, if lenders charge 1 percent interest each month, the APR is a straightforward 12 percent (1 percent x 12 months = 12 percent). In mortgages, it is the interest rate of a mortgage, taking into account the interest, mortgage insurance and certain closing costs including points paid at closing.

Fees typically included in an APR calculation		
Points—all Discount and Origination fees/points.	Prepaid Interest—companies may use any number between one and 30 days of interest.	Credit card insurance—insurance that pays off the amount owed in the event of the borrower's death.
Loan processing fee.	Documentation preparation fee.	Private mortgage insurance.
Loan application fee.	Underwriting fee.	

If you carry a part of your balance from month-to-month, even a small difference in the APR can make a big difference in how much you will pay over the life of the loan.

Different Types of APR

A fixed-rate APR does not change from month to month. A variable rate APR changes from period to period (that may be month-to-month or day-to-day). The rate is usually tied to another interest rate, such as the prime rate or the Treasury bill rate. If the other rate changes, the rate on your card may change, too.

The finance charge is the dollar amount you pay in exchange for the privilege to secure credit. The amount depends in part on your outstanding balance and the APR.

Credit card companies use one of several methods to calculate an outstanding balance. The method used can make a big difference in the amount of finance charge you pay. Your outstanding balance may be calculated:

- Over one billing cycle or two;
- using the adjusted balance, the average daily balance or the previous balance; and
- including or excluding new purchases in the balance.

Depending on the balance you carry and the timing of your purchases and payments, you will have a lower finance charge with one-cycle billing and either:

- The average daily balance method excluding new purchases;
- the adjusted balance method; or
- the previous balance method.

Minimum Finance Charge

Most credit cards have a minimum finance charge policy. You will be charged a minimum finance fee even if the calculated amount of your finance charge is less. For example, your finance charge may be calculated to be 35 cents, but if the company's minimum finance charge is $1, you will be charged $1. A minimum finance charge usually applies only when you carry over a balance from one billing cycle to the next.

APR vs. APY

How does APY work differently than APR? They sound similar but are very different. APY (annual percentage yield) is the effective annual rate of return that takes into account the effect of compounding interest. The APY for a 1 percent rate of interest compounded monthly adds up to 12.68 percent a year. If you carry a balance on your credit card for only 1 month, with an APR you would be charge for 1 month's period (1 percent). However, if you carry a balance from one month to the next, your effective APY interest rate becomes 12.68 percent as a result of the compounding each month.

The APY is based on the assumption that funds will remain in a chosen account for a full 365 days and will not be moved about. Both APR and APY calculations are used in determining a return on investment and interest paid.

Comparing each value reveals how APY and APR differs:

Investor A purchases a bond for $1,000 that pays 6 percent APY upon maturity.

Investor B places the same amount into a money market account for the same time period that pays .05 percent per month APR.

After 12 months Investor A will have earned a compounded yield of 6.17 percent of ($61.70), while Investor B will have earned a regular 6 percent yield or $60). The return on investment for this example is small, but the differences with larger amounts of money over a longer period can become quite significant.

The Solution

Finally, many lenders are completely unaware of what is included in their APR because they use software programs to compute their APRs. It is quite possible that the same lender with the same interest rate may include different charges in the equation to arrive at two different APRs. The best advice, then, is to use the APR as a starting point only to compare loans. Ask your lender to itemize fees included in the APR and follow these tips:

- An APR does not tell you how long your rate is locked for. A lender who offers you a 10-day rate lock may have a lower APR than a lender who offers you a 60-day rate lock, so ask your lender if a shorter lock will lower your interest rate.
- Calculating APRs on adjustable and balloon loans is very complex because future rates are unknown. The result is even more confusion about how lenders calculate APRs.
- Do not compare a 30-year loan with a 15-year loan using the respective APRs. A 15-year loan may have a lower interest rate, but could have a higher APR since the loan fees are amortized over a shorter period of time.

The Resources

www.finance-encyclopedia.com/tem/apr

For a definition of APR from a financial encyclopedia.

www.investopedia.com

Learn more about APRs, including a comprehensive investing dictionary and financial tutorials and articles.

www.efunda.com/formulae/finance/apr_calculator.cfm

For a useful tool to calculate the APR for loans with added costs.

28

To Lease or Not to Lease

The Challenge

Which is best, to lease or buy? Leases and loans are simply two different methods of automobile financing. One finances the use of a vehicle, the other finances the purchase of a vehicle. Each option is full of benefits and drawbacks. Which is better depends upon your personal priorities and financial resources. Is having a new vehicle every 2 or 3 years with no major repair risks more important than long-term cost savings? Are long-term cost savings more important than lower monthly payments? Is ownership more important than low up-front costs versus no down payment? In any case, operating a car can be expensive as gasoline, scheduled maintenance, surprise repairs, insurance and registrations add up. In this chapter we will compare the emotional and financial benefits of leasing versus buying to help you choose the best option for your lifestyle.

The Facts

The comparison chart shows the advantages to leasing and buying.

Buying vs. Leasing Comparison

Buying	Leasing
Larger down payment lowers monthly payments. Large down payment ties up investment money.	Lower or no down payment so money can be invested elsewhere.
Buyer pays full tax on full purchase price of the car minus trade-in allowance.	Lower sales tax (tax is only paid on the amount of the car's value during the lease term).
Car is under full warranty 24 to 36 months. The loan may extend for 36 to 60 months.	Car is under full warranty during the term of the 24 to 36 month lease.
No mileage restrictions.	Drive more than the pre-set maximum number of miles and you will be assessed a per mile over-the-limit penalty.

May keep car for as long as you want.	Trade in for a new car every 3 years.
You pay for the full-price of the car.	You only pay a portion of the full price of the car.
Higher payments limit the amount of car you can buy.	Lower payments let you buy more car for the money.
If car is stolen you may owe more than the car is worth.	Gap coverage, or gap insurance, pays the difference between what you owe on your loan or lease, and what your vehicle is actually worth if your vehicle is stolen or destroyed.
You build equity with each loan payment.	You do not build any equity during the term of the lease.
You are responsible for car scheduled maintenance and general upkeep including brakes, muffler, oil changes, etc. and insurance coverage.	You are responsible for car scheduled maintenance and general upkeep including brakes, muffler, oil changes, etc. and insurance coverage.
When you are ready to sell the car you must trade it in or sell it yourself.	At the end of the lease you turn the car in.

Visit *www.encouragementpress.com* to view the chart showing the financial comparisons between buying vs. leasing a car.

Automobile leases are generally of two varieties: closed-end and open-end. There is a big difference between the two types and you should understand that difference before you sign your lease contract. Federal regulations require that the type of lease be clearly indicated on all lease contracts.

Closed-end leases, sometimes called walk-away leases, are the most common type of consumer leases today. With this type of lease you simply return your vehicle at the end of the lease and will have no other responsibilities other than paying for excessive damage or over the limit mileage charges. The typical closed-end lease limits the number of miles you drive annually to 12,000.

Open-end leases are primarily for commercial business leasing. In this case the lessee, not the leasing company, takes all the financial risks, which is not so much a problem for a business, since the cost can be expensed. Annual mileage on a business lease is usually much greater than 12,000 miles.

Lease vs. Buy?
- The short-term monthly cost of leasing is always significantly less than the cost of buying. For the same car, same price, same term and same down payment, monthly lease payments will always be 30 to 60 percent lower than loan payments. This is still true even when compared to zero percent

or low-interest loans.

- The medium-term cost of leasing is about the same as the cost of buying, assuming the buyer sells/trades his or her vehicle at the end of the loan.
- The long-term cost of leasing is always more than the cost of buying, assuming the buyer keeps the vehicle. The reason is the cost of depreciation is figured into monthly lease payments. The longer you lease the car, the higher your payments will be because the car is worth less at the end of the lease term.

The price for the car you agree upon with the dealer is referred to as the *capitalized cost*, or *cap cost* or *lease cost*. If you are a skilled negotiator the cap cost can end up being significantly less than the Manufacturers Suggested Retail Price (MSRP). While not specified in lease contracts, capitalized costs may include acquisition fees (similar to mortgage points or loan origination fees). You can reduce caps costs by taking advantage of rebates, factory-to-dealer incentives, trade-in credits or a cash-down payment. These reductions are known as *cap cost reductions*. Deducting cap cost reductions from the cap cost equals the *net capitalized cost*, sometimes called *adjusted cap cost*.

The wholesale value of a car at the end of its lease term, after it has depreciated, is called its *residual value*. Residuals are usually stated as a percentage of MSRP. A 36-month, 50 percent residual on a new $20,000 car means that its estimated depreciated value at the end of a 3-year lease will be $10,000. The best cars to lease are those whose 24-month residuals are at least 50 percent of their original MSRP value.

When you lease, you are charged interest just as if you had purchased the car. This interest is expressed as a money factor, sometimes called *lease factor* or simply *factor* and is specified as a small number such as .00297. The money factor is easily converted to an annual interest rate (APR) by multiplying by 2400 (not related to the lease length). For example, a money factor of .00297 multiplied by 2400 = 7.13 percent.

Lease money factors, converted to APR, should be comparable to, if not lower than, local new-car loan interest rates.

Typical leases are 24, 36, or 48 months. Odd term leases such as 30, 39 and 42 months are frequently seen in lease promotional ads. A shorter-term lease is more expensive than a longer-term lease. Although longer leases produce somewhat lower monthly payments, it may be smarter to choose a lease term that is equal to the coverage warranty that comes with your vehicle. That way, you are covered for the entire duration of the lease if something breaks.

The Solution

Buy or lease? That is the question and it can only be answered based on your preferences and lifestyle. Purchasing a car may result in higher monthly payments for a fixed term. At the end of the loan term you will own the car, payment free. There are no mile restrictions and you do not have to be extra careful to make sure you are trading in a car in good condition.

If you like to drive a new car every few years, like the smell of a new car and drive fewer than 12,000 miles a year, leasing may be a better option for you. If you choose to lease these tips will help you get the best deal.

- It is always in your best interest to negotiate the lowest capitalized cost just as if you were buying. The lower your cap cost, the lower your monthly lease payments will be.
- The higher the residual value, the more the car is worth at lease-end–and the lower your lease payments.
- Like interest on a loan, the lower the money factor, the lower your monthly lease payments. The money factor and interest rate is not required to be shown in lease contracts. So, if you want to know your money factor, you will have to ask.
- Choose a lease term that is equal to the coverage warranty that comes with your vehicle. That way you are covered for the entire duration of the lease if something breaks.
- And finally, always go with a closed-end lease and never an open-end lease.

The Resources

For more in-depth information about leasing, visit these Websites:

www.fundadvice.com/tools/calculator/

This calculator lets you compare buying a car vs. leasing.

www.edmunds.com/advice/buying/articles/4707/article.html

Compare the costs of buying vs. leasing vs. buying a used vehicle.

www.newbuyer.com/autoleasing/whattobuy/leasevsbuy.htm

New Buyers Leasing Guide.

www.automotive.com/auto-loans/36/loan-tips/car-leasing-vs-car-buying.html
www.leaseguide.com/lease03.htm

Informative guides to leasing a car.

29

Should You Rent or Buy a Home?

The Challenge

Virtually every rent versus buy calculator will show you that it is more advantageous to buy a home than to rent. The advantages to buying go beyond just financial rewards: buying enables you to build equity, there are tax savings to be had with home ownership and best of all, there are no rules so you can customize your space any way you like. The tax benefits aside there are other factors to consider:

- Do you want to pay on a mortgage for the next 15 to 30 years?
- Do you prefer to have the mortgage holder keep your tax and insurance escrow and be responsible for paying them for you?
- Do you plan on staying put for the next 5 to 10 years?
- Are home values in your area projected to increase or decrease during the next 5 years?

The decision to buy or rent is usually made based on financial or convenience factors. Retirees report that after so many years of owning and dealing with maintenance issues on a home, they like the idea of calling the landlord to report problems. That is why they pay rent. The problem becomes the landlord's, not theirs. Other retirees like the security of knowing they own the property, can decorate to their tastes and can pass the property onto their heirs.

Owning a home is never cheap, and while the financial benefits to owning are not the most important, they are significant and should be weighed. In this chapter we will take a closer look at financial advantages and disadvantages to renting or buying to help you decide which option is best for you.

The Facts

First, let us take a look the advantages and disadvantages of owning and renting.

Renting Advantages	Buying Disadvantages
Fixed cost for term of lease. Lease rate may increase faster than rate of inflation.	Taxes, maintenance and upkeep costs may vary.
Utility costs may be included in the monthly lease.	Utilities are charged separately and may vary each month.
When the lease ends you are free to move with little notice and a light cleaning.	To move you must prepare your home for sale and get it sold. Costs may be required to complete the sale.
Landlord is responsible for maintenance, painting and upkeep. Have a problem? Call the landlord.	You are responsible for maintenance, painting and upkeep. Have a problem? Call your handyman or roll up your sleeves and get to work.
Smaller, up-front deposit amount required. You can invest your money elsewhere.	Large cash outlay needed for down payment.

Renting Disadvantages	Buying Advantages
Your landlord builds equity while you pay to rent the property.	You build equity with each monthly payment. Eventually you will own the property.
If you personalize your apartment with paint or window treatments you must restore the walls to white or you may forfeit your deposit. Any window treatments generally stay with the unit when you leave.	You may remodel and redecorate your home to match your taste and needs.
There are no tax advantages given to the renter. The landlord gets any and all tax breaks.	Taxes and interest are deductible on your income taxes. Other tax breaks may be available.
Landlord may not renew the lease.	You can stay as long as you pay the mortgage/taxes.

Now, let us review the financial benefits of buying versus renting.

If you pay your $50,000 mortgage off in 15 years, you will save $94,921 compared to renting. During those same years, if you had paid $1,000 a month rent, you would have paid your landlord a total of $180,000 in rent (with or without utilities included). During the same 15 years you would have paid $174,285 to own. Plus, your monthly mortgage payments would have been less each month than your monthly rent.

$138,960	taxes, principal, interest and insurance
+ $30,000	maintenance costs
+ $27,430	selling fees
$196,390	
$22,105	difference in tax savings
$174,285	

The cost to own is even less if you subtract the increased value of the home ($141,858) at the time it was sold from the cost to own ($174,285). The total cost to own would be further reduced to $32,700.

Your savings breakdown is as follows:

Tax savings:	$22,105
Maintenance costs:	$30,000
Original purchase Price:	$250,000
Original mortgage amount:	$50,000
Selling Price:	$391,858
Equity gained:	$141,858
Selling Costs*:	$27,430

*(Includes realtor fees and other fees. Percentages may vary based on fees charged in your area.)

The Solution

Short of moving in with one of your children, you have two housing options—you can rent or you can buy. As illustrated above, the benefits of owning almost always financially out-weigh renting. However, there are more factors to consider than just finances. The decision to rent or to buy depends on your lifestyle, the strength or weakness of the rental or selling market in your area, how much money you have saved for retirement, and your own personal preferences.

If your home is paid off, you may consider selling to unlock the equity in the home or, depending on interest rates, open an equity line of credit to pull out the cash as needed. If the market is strong, you may get top dollar for your home. The benefits to owning are that you have the power to borrow against the value of your home and the interest paid on the loan is tax deductible. This is one strategy to reducing the taxable amount of your estate.

If the housing market is weak, it may take longer for you to sell your home and you may make less profit. If this is the case, the rental market is probably hot, meaning you will pay more for a rental. Holding off selling until the housing market improves may be the best strategy.

If you have not saved enough or earned a lower than expected return on your investments, you may need to pull the equity from your home to meet your retirement expenses. Again, selling your largest asset, investing the money and renting for a while may be the best solution.

If you like the idea of someone else being responsible for upkeep and maintenance, having your utilities included in your monthly rent or the flexibility of being able to pack up and move at any time, renting might just be the thing for you.

Owning a home is an investment and requires financial resources to keep the home in top condition. The key to successful and happy home ownership is having those resources available so you do not become mortgage poor and worry about keeping the house up and keeping it out of the hands of the bank or the tax man.

The Resources

www.freddiemac.com

> Feddie Mac Website offers excellent calculators, worksheets and cost estimating tools to help renters become home buyers and home buyers get more for their money.

Other online calculators can be found by visiting the following sites:

www.tcalc.com/tvwww.dll?LoanVsLoan?Tmplt=RentVsBuy2.htm&Cstm=frs_home&blnPmt1=60&Usr1=800.00

> Calculator compares rental costs vs. the real cost of buying a home, including taxes, fees, and interest, but not payments made against the principal on your loan, since those payments become equity in your home.

www.homeadvisor.com

www.eloan.com

www.homefair.com/homefair/servlet/ActionServlet?pid=27&cid=homefair

www.newbuyer.com/homes/homeguide/deciding/rentvsbuythm

> For an article discussing whether renting or buying makes sense for you.

30
To Mortgage or Reverse Mortgage?

The Challenge

Until recently there were two ways to get cash from your home: sell it or borrow against it. Recent trends show that more retirees want to stay in their homes as long as possible after retirement.

The challenge for retirees is to tap into their home's equity without selling the house or taking on the burden of a loan that must be repaid. There are three ways this can be accomplished:

1. Sell the home and move to a smaller home or condo.
2. Open an equity line of credit or home loan against the equity in the home.
3. Take out a reverse mortgage.

Depending on your circumstances, a reverse mortgage may be the answer for you.

The Facts

The Reverse Mortgage

A reverse mortgage is a loan against your home that you do not have to pay back as long as you live in the home. A reverse mortgage turns the value of your home into cash that is paid to you through:

- A credit line account that lets you decide when and how much of the available cash is paid to you.
- A single lump sum payment.
- Regular monthly cash advances.
- A combination of these payouts.

It is important to note that a reverse mortgage is a loan agreement, but the loan does not need to be repaid until you die, sell the home or permanently move out of your home (vacant for 12 months). To be eligible for most reverse mortgages, you must own your home, be 62 years or older and the home must be mortgage or loan free. With a reverse mortgage you remain the owner of your home so you are still responsible for paying your property taxes, maintain and repair your home and keep your home insured. You may be considered in default of your agreement if you fail to keep the property in good condition, declare bankruptcy or donate or abandon your home.

One stipulation for qualifying for a reverse mortgage is it must be the first mortgage, that is, it must be the primary debt against your home. If you owe any money on your property you must:

- Pay off the old debt before you get a reverse mortgage and
- pay off the old debt with the money you get from a reserve mortgage.

As with any loan, it is important to understand the terms of the loan. The debt you owe on a mortgage includes all loan advances you receive, any finance loan costs, interest from the loan, as well as loan origination and servicing fees. The total annual loan cost (TALC) combines all of a reverse mortgage's costs into a single annual average rate. This information is useful when comparing one type of reverse mortgage to another. But it also shows how individual reverse mortgage loans can vary from one company to another. It also lets you know how much the loans may end up costing you, which can be more than you might have originally thought. AARP provides a calculator (*www.aarp.com/talc*) that lets you calculate your TALC.

A Home Equity Conversion Mortgage (HECM) is the only reverse mortgage insured by the federal government. HECM loans are issued by the Federal Housing Administration (FHA). The FHA controls how much HECM lenders can lend you based on your age and home value and limits how much you will pay in loan costs.

The amount of cash you can take depends on your age, current interest rates and your home's value. The older you are, the more cash you can get, since the loan is based on your life expectancy. If there is more than one owner, the age of the youngest homeowner is the one that counts.

The greater the home's appraised value the more money you can qualify for, but there are limits on the total amount of money you can get. If your home is worth more than the limit for your area, you are still eligible for the loan but the amount you can take is based on your county limit, not on your home's actual value.

This table shows how much you can take based on your age and home value. Visit *www.encouragementpress.com* to view the HECM table displaying home value, age and qualifying amounts.

HECM Costs

Nothing in life is cheap, and neither is a HECM loan. The itemized costs of a HECM include an origination fee, third-party closing costs, a mortgage insurance premium, a servicing fee and interest.

- The origination fee is charged by the lender for preparing your paperwork and processing your loan. HECM regulations limit the origination fee to 2 percent of your home's value or county limit. For example, on a $350,000 home the origination fee could be as high as $7,000. This fee may be negotiated by some lenders.
- Third-party closing costs may be based on the value of your home or by area. HECM insurance is financed by a Mortgage Insurance Premium (MIP) charged on all HECM loans. The cost is charged in two parts:
  - Two percent of your home's value or the limit in your area, whichever is less.
  - One-half percent is added to the interest rate charged on your loan balance.

The MIP guarantees that your total debt can never be greater than the value of your home.

- Servicing fees are charged monthly and covers everything a lender does after closing to make sure everything is administered correctly as you requested, such as transferring premiums to FHA, paying property taxes and insurance premiums and monitoring your compliance with your obligations under the loan agreement. The amount is limited to a maximum of $35 a month.
- Your interest rate is usually adjustable on HECM loans with an annual cap of 2 percentage points and an over-the-life-of-the-loan cap of 5 points. Interest is tied to the current 1-year U.S. Treasury Security rate. This means the rate may go up or down every year.

Other types of reverse mortgages include:

- Deferred Payment Loans (DPLs) are given for the sole purpose of making repairs or improving the home. This type of loan is a one-time, lump sum loan. No repayment is required as long as you live in your home. This type of loan is limited to homeowners with low or moderate incomes, and some lenders have age or disability requirements. Only specific types of repairs or improvements may be made with DLP loans, such as a new roof, wiring, heating, plumbing, floors, stairs, porches, ramps or other disability improvements. Interest is often fixed and simple interest is charged.
- Property Tax Deferral Loans (PTD) provides annual loan advances that can be used only to pay your property taxes. Loan repayment is not required

as long as you live in the home. The loan amount is usually limited to the amount of your taxes due for the year. The total amount you can borrow over the life of the PTD is limited and you may become ineligible for future loan advances at some point. Not all states offer PTDs so check with your local government agency for availability.

- Proprietary reverse mortgages are almost always the most expensive type of reverse mortgage, but if your home is worth more than HUDs limits for your county then one of these loans might provide larger cash advances than a HECM.

Monthly Payments

For a 75-year old borrower living in a $250,000 home who takes a $40,000 combination loan consisting of a $20,000 lump sum and $20,000 credit line at a 7 percent interest, the borrower would receive a $697 lifetime monthly payment or $875 over 15 years, or $1,120 over 10 years, or $1,891 over 5 years. The chart shows the difference in amounts paid over various time periods.

	As long as you live in your home	15 years	10 years	5 years
	$991	$1,243	$1,592	$2,688
20,000	$844	$1,059	$1,356	$2,289
40,000	$697	$875	$1,120	$1,891
60,000	$550	$690	$884	$1,493
80,000	$403	$506	$648	$1,094
100,000	$256	$322	$412	$696
120,000	$110	$138	$176	$298
134,984	$0	$0	$0	$0

The Solution

Every situation is different and it is important you discuss your individual situation with a qualified professional and your family before making the final decision. As with all your retirement planning, do the math to make sure your decision is the best one for your lifestyle.

The Resources

www.elderloan.com/
www.ftc.gov/bcp/conline/pubs/homes/rms.htm

For further information on reverse mortgages and other types of home loans.

31

Refinancing Your Home–
Best Times &
Best Programs

The Challenge

Along with the dream of home ownership is the dream of paying off your mortgage before you retire. The one tid-bit of financial advice passed from generation to generation has been to pay off your home before you retire. Not so fast, say some financial planners. The retirement rules of yesterday may no longer apply to the lifestyles of today.

The first thing you as a homeowner need to do before paying down or paying off the mortgage is to weigh your potential returns. Should you pay off your mortgage? If you pay off your mortgage early you will lose one of the few remaining tax write-offs still allowed–mortgage interest. If you are in the 30 percent federal-tax bracket, paying off a mortgage with a 6 percent interest rate provides a 4.2 percent rate of return after taxes, mostly in part due to the tax deduction on mortgage interest.

There are three main reasons why it is worthwhile to refinance.

1. You may be able to cut interest costs by lowering your rate. Traditionally, the rule of thumb has been that it only makes sense to refinance if you get a rate that is 1 percent to 2 percent lower than you are currently paying. But new financing options have changed the rules. Lenders offering low cost or no cost loans make it profitable to refinance even at a half percent discount. Carefully review the terms and costs of recently advertised no cost loans.

2. A different loan may fit your current financial situation better. If you have an adjustable rate loan you may be squeezed by steadily rising interest rates. A fixed-rate loan with predictable payments may be a better fit for you.

3. It may be time to cash-out the equity locked up in your home. With a cash-out refinance, you adjust your total mortgage higher and pocket the difference. For example, if you owe $60,000 on your current home loan and need $20,000 cash for medical or home repairs, you may get a better

rate on a $80,000 mortgage while keeping $20,000 cash. Tapping home equity is a good way to pay for college, remodeling or a new car. But keep in mind with a cash-out you still pay closing costs and other fees. And, of course, it will not be worth it if your new interest rate ends up being higher than your current rate.

The Facts

The new general rule of thumb, if your current home mortgage interest rate is at least one-half a point above the new interest rate you could receive, then refinancing would be a good choice.

You can refinance home mortgage loans to:

- Reduce your monthly payments by taking advantage of lower interest rates.
- Avoid the risk of higher interest payments in the future by switching from an adjustable-rate mortgage to a fixed-rate home mortgage loan or from a balloon home mortgage to a fixed-rate mortgage.
- Reduce your interest cost over the life of your mortgage by taking advantage of lower rates or shortening the term of your loan.
- Increase your total assets available for retirement planning by paying off your home mortgage faster (accelerating the build-up of home equity), or free up cash for major expenses such as long term care or remodeling your home.
- Reduce expenses with debt consolidation loans by paying off high interest, high cost credit card debt with the cash from a home mortgage refinance.
- Lower your taxes by exchanging non-tax deductible credit card or car loan debt for tax-deductible home equity debt.

Home mortgage refinancing is not without risk. Be careful of:

- Increasing your loan amount when refinancing a home. If you increase the amount of your home mortgage by cashing out home equity, you increase your financial risk due to the larger debt amount and, possibly, the longer term on your loan.
- Selecting risky loan terms. There are a number of ways to structure a loan and some of these strategies can leave you open to a lot of risk. For example, if you use an adjustable rate mortgage or a home equity line of credit that has a variable interest rate, then your monthly payments will rise if interest rates go up.
- Mortgage refinancing closing costs outweighing savings. Because there are transaction costs to refinancing a home, there is a risk that if your gains from mortgage refinancing are small, these will not outweigh the closing costs on taking the new home loan.

- Refinancing with a 30-year loan while in your 50s. If you do so, you may be paying a monthly mortgage well into retirement.
- Not paying off a home mortgage when you have a very low interest rate. The tax benefits for low mortgage interest rates are limited and paying off your mortgage may be advantageous as you might be able make more by investing somewhere else, such as stocks, bonds or CDs.

The Solution

When refinancing your mortgage, you will want to understand:

- Your own goals. How long do you plan to stay in the home? What is your current interest rate? What is your credit rating? Different loan features will meet the different needs of each household. The type of financing you select depends on your financial goals.
- The various loan fees. Closing costs are miscellaneous costs associated with your closing a real estate transaction and may include attorney fees, appraisals, credit reports, prepaid interest, title insurance, recording fees, homeowner's insurance and transfer taxes.
- Cost of points. Paying points means you are paying some money upfront in exchange for lower monthly payments and/or a lower interest rate. Points are expressed as a percentage of the loan amount. If you are paying three points you are paying a charge equal to 3 percent of the loan balance.
- The loan terms. How long do you intend to stay in your house? Short-term loans will usually offer lower interest rates than long-term loans. Short-term loans are generally adjustable rate loans while long-term loans are generally fixed-rate loans.
- The loan marketplace. Shop around! Obtain at least three loan quotes to make sure that you get the best loan terms and are not paying too much in closing costs.
- Know who your lender is. Is your lender a prime or sub-prime lender? Sub-prime lenders often offer financing at a higher interest rate to borrowers who have poor or no credit. Prime lenders offer loans just a 1 or 2 percentage rates above prime.

Finally, the best strategy you can employ when looking for home mortgage refinancing is to educate yourself.

- Learn about the pros and cons of different mortgage features and restrictions. Understanding how different features, like points, will affect your particular situation is extremely important.
- Do the math to determine if refinancing is cost effective for you.
- Shop around to find the best loan program for your lifestyle. Always compare several different quotes from multiple home mortgage lenders.

- Be aware of who is granting the loan. Are you getting a loan from a prime or sub-prime lender?
- Watch out for mortgage refinance loan programs that may switch to a higher rate later on in the term of the loan.
- Do not let a loan officer talk you into borrowing more than you truly need. The more you borrow, the higher your borrowing costs will be.

Consider refinancing carefully, particularly if you are closer to retirement. Your needs may evolve over the next few years. The length of time you intend to stay in the house can help you determine whether refinancing a home or taking out a reverse mortgage is a good fit for your situation. For example, if you intend to move in the near future, refinancing (and the upfront closing costs to refinance home mortgage loans) may not be a good strategy for you. On the other hand, if you believe that you will remain in your house for a long time, then refinancing or a reverse mortgage may be a great option, and paying points up front could offer great cost savings with a lower interest rate over the long-term. This can be a great way to unlock some of the equity you have built up in your home.

The Resources

To take advantage of refinance calculators, visit:

www.truecredit.com
www.bankrate.com
www.*realestatejournal.com*
www.tcalc.com/tvwww.dll?LoanVsLoan
www.weatrust.com/calc/MortgageRefinance.html

http://efinancedirectorycom/index.html

User-friendly directory of original articles, tips and other resources.

www.newretirement.com/Services/Mortgage_Refinancing.aspx

A Website dedicated to helping people who are concerned about retirement find the information they need to create a secure future for themselves.

32

Home Equity Loans—
The Ins & Outs

The Challenge

An increasing number of retirees are still paying mortgages. Today, more than 30 percent of homeowners 65 and older still carry a mortgage balance of $30,000 or more. The monthly payment, although tending to be lower, can still eat up a significant portion of a retiree's fixed monthly income. Data published by the Federal Reserve in early 2006 shows that mortgage debt by all ages grew by 75 percent over the past 5 years, outpacing the 71 percent growth in the value of household real estate.

Retirees are also tapping into home equity to generate spending money. As a result, debt is rising. According to the Federal Reserve's 2004 Survey of Consumer Finances, 40 percent of households headed by someone aged 75 or older had debt in 2004, up from 29 percent in 2001. Not only are many people still paying off the mortgages on their primary residences, but some of them have purchased vacation homes, taking on second mortgages. The U.S. Census Bureau cited 6.6 million vacation homes in the U.S. in 2003. The typical vacation home buyer, according to the National Association of Realtors, is aged 55 or older.

Is carrying a small mortgage really a bad idea? Deducting interest on a primary residence is one of the few tax deductions still available today. Tapping into the equity of a paid-in-full million dollar home may provide the owner with additional tax deductible income and reduce the value of the estate. The challenge is determining when it is beneficial to tap into the equity of your home or if purchasing a new home and keeping a small mortgage is the right financial strategy for your lifestyle.

The Facts

A home-equity loan, also known as a second mortgage, lets homeowners borrow money by leveraging the equity in their homes. Home-equity loans exploded in popularity in 1996, providing consumers a mean to circumvent that year's tax changes, which eliminated deductions for the interest on most consumer purchases. With a home-equity loan, homeowners can borrow up to $100,000 and still deduct all of the interest when they file their tax returns.

Home equity loans come in two varieties: fixed-rate or variable rate home equity lines of credit. Both types are available with terms that generally range from 5 to 15 years. Both types of loans must be repaid in full if the home on which they are borrowing from is sold.

Fixed-rate loans provide a single, lump-sum payment to the borrower, which is repaid over a set period of time at an agreed-upon interest rate. The payment and interest rate remain the same over the lifetime of the loan.

A Home-Equity Line of Credit (HELOC) is a variable-rate loan that works much like a credit card. Borrowers are pre-approved for a certain spending limit and can withdraw money when they need it via a credit card or special checks. Monthly payments vary based on the amount of money borrowed and the current interest rate. Like fixed-rate loans, the HELOC has a set term length. The borrower may repay the loan and borrow the full amount again as often as he or she wishes during the term of the loan. However, when the end of the term is reached, the outstanding loan amount must be repaid in full or rolled over into a new loan.

Home-equity loans provide an easy source of cash. The interest rate on a home-equity loan—although higher than that of a first mortgage—is much lower than on credit cards and other consumer loans. The number one reason consumers borrow against the value of their homes via a fixed-rate home equity loan is to pay off credit or car loans. By consolidating debt with the home-equity loan, you get a single payment, a lower interest rate and tax benefits.

Home-equity loans can produce a big benefit for the lender. If you default on the loan, the lender gets to keep all the money earned on the initial mortgage and all the money earned on the home-equity loan. Additionally, the lender gets to repossess your property, sell it again and restart the cycle with the next borrower.

Home-equity loans can benefit borrowers too. If you have a steady, reliable source of income and know that you will be able to repay the loan, the low interest rate and tax deductibility of paid interest makes it a good borrowing choice. Fixed-rate home-equity loans can help cover the cost of a single, large purchase, such a new roof on your home or an unexpected medical bill. And the HELOC provides a convenient way to cover short-term, recurring costs, such as the quarterly tuition for a college degree.

The main pitfall associated with any home-equity loan is that they are a relatively easy solution for a homeowner who may have difficulty curbing their spending. The phrase *reloading* has been given to homeowners who borrow to pay off other credit and then rack up the debt on the credit cards again before paying off the line of credit. If you take out a line of credit that is higher than the value of your home, you will pay higher fees and the interest paid on the portion of the loan that is above the value of the home is not tax deductible.

If you are nearing retirement age you need to determine how the loan may affect your ability to reach your income goals. Would you be able to repay a loan on a fixed income if interest rates climb from 4.5 percent to 7.5 percent in the course of a year?

The Solution

It may be tempting to open a home equity line of credit to splurge on expensive luxuries. Before you borrow against your home, conduct a careful review of your financial situation. Make sure that you understand the terms of the loan and have the means to make the payments without compromising other bills and comfortably repay the debt on or before its due date.

If your home is paid off, a home equity loan may give you a larger monthly income while reducing the size of your estate. You must repay the loan, however, and with increasing interest rates that may be tough.

If you have large medical bills to pay or other unexpected expenses, a line of credit is much cheaper than a regular bank loan or financing the purchase with the company. It will also provide you with a tax deduction that will reduce your tax liability on your annual income.

When interest rates are low (4 percent), it may make sense to take out small loans. You get an interest deduction and you may be able to invest that money somewhere else, such as an annuity guaranteeing 5 percent.

When rates on a credit line rise, long-term mortgage rates generally fall. This up-down combination gives you a chance to pay off your credit line with another type of loan that may have a lower interest rate. One of the major drawbacks to a variable line of credit is your monthly payments may increase as the prime lending rate increases each month. If the interest rate on a line of credit becomes higher than a fixed-rate mortgage, you may want to consider refinancing your home. You can take a small amount of equity for a lower rate than a variable loan.

The Resources

www.bankrate.com

To determine whether a loan or a line of credit is better for you.

33

Is Early Retirement an Option?

The Challenge

Have you ever dreamed of retiring early? We all have. At some point in your working career, you have probably dreamed of retiring to your own private tropical island, sipping a cool drink while watching the waves roll in and out. Wake up! That only happens in commercials. The reality is that you would have to be a very savvy investor, have won the lottery or have inherited a big estate to make your dreams come true (at least the private island part).

Although a topical island may not be possible, taking early retirement is. In fact, anything is possible, it just takes planning, planning and more planning to make your dreams come true. In this chapter we will discuss two challenges you may face if taking early retirement. The first is planning your early retirement so you can live comfortably and ensure you have enough income in your accounts to support you for many years. The second is preparing emotionally for a change socially.

The Facts

If you want to retire early or if you are in serious financial straits and need to tap into your IRA money, there is a way to do it without triggering a penalty. If you take money out of an IRA before age 59½, you usually have to pay a 10 percent penalty on top of ordinary income taxes. However, there is an exception to these penalties if you take the money out in substantially equal payments over your lifetime. IRS rules require that you take at least one payment annually for the exception to apply. Actuarial tables are used to determine life expectancy and, in essence, you are turning your retirement plan into an annuity (also called an annuity distribution), or annuitizing an IRA. Again, the key is to take payouts on a specific schedule. This method allows you to begin withdrawing from your IRA early, but the amount is determined by an IRS calculated life-expectancy table (see Chapter 38: *Special IRA Allowances*).

Taking an early withdrawal is not popular or necessarily a good idea for several reasons. This is best illustrated through an example. If you have $100,00 in an IRA account and you decided to take distribution payments early–say age 55–you would have to take $3,500 a year for 28.6 years. This severely limits the ability for this money to grow. If for any reason should you decide that taking the distribution was a bad decision and want to reduce the payment to $2,000, the IRS would hit you with a 10 percent penalty. IRS rules state that you cannot change the payment plan for 5 years or until you reach age 59½, whichever is later.

But where it does make sense to take an annuity distribution payment on a retirement plan is:

- If you are in your 50s or early 60s and lost your job or became ill. While this is not exactly the early retirement you might have envisioned, if there is a substantial amount of money in the IRA, an annuity distribution can be set up. At age 55 your estimated life expectancy is 28.6 years. If you have a $500,000 IRA, the pay out for the one-life annuity, at equal payments for 28.6 years, would be approximately $17,483.
- If you wanted to reduce your estate size to minimize your tax liability before required minimum distributions must be taken or want to pay less taxes each month on a smaller distribution amount while in a lower tax bracket. (See Chapter 37: *Retirement Withdrawal Rules*.)

To emphasize an important point again, early-withdrawal exceptions do not eliminate your tax bill if you take the money out of a traditional IRA. Contributions to IRAs are pre-tax, meaning taxes have not been deducted from your earning and that makes them tax-deferred investments. Taxes are paid when withdrawals begin. Roth accounts, however, are funded with after-tax dollars, meaning taxes have already been deducted from your earnings. You are taxed on the interest earned only from Roth accounts. So when you take the money out of a traditional IRA, regardless of your age or the purpose of the withdrawal, you will owe your regular tax rate on the amount withdrawn.

You must inform the IRS that you used the retirement money early for a tax-acceptable purpose by filing IRS *Form 5329*. When you fill out the form you will also enter a code, found in the form's instructions. This form lets the IRS know the distribution is penalty free.

Of course, all this is assuming you are taking distributions from a private retirement account. The rules are different if you plan to collect Social Security earlier than your designated full retirement age. If you were born after 1937, you can start your Social Security retirement benefits as early as age 62, but the reduction in benefit amount will depend on the year you were born. The maximum reduction at age 62 will be 25 percent for people who reach age 62 in 2005, and 30 percent for people born after 1959.

If you start your benefits early, they will be permanently reduced based on the number of months you receive benefits before you reach your full retirement age. If you wait until you reach your full retirement age to collect benefits, you will receive the full amount.

Social Security benefits are decreased by a certain percentage (depending on your date of birth) if you take distribution payments before you reach full retirement age. Reduced retirement benefits, if taken at age 62, are about 30 percent less than if taken at full retirement age. The reduction for starting benefits at age:

- 63 is about 25 percent;
- 64 is about 20 percent;
- 65 is about 13.3 percent; and
- 66 is about 6.7 percent.

If you collect early, at age 62, your spouse's benefits will be affected too. Benefit as a spouse at 62 is about 67.5 percent of the benefit your spouse would receive if his or her benefits started at full retirement age. The reduction for starting benefits as a spouse at age:

- 63 is about 65 percent;
- 64 is about 62.5 percent;
- 65 is about 58.3 percent;
- 66 is about 54.2 percent; and
- 67 is 50 percent.

What is the best age to start your retirement benefits? You must weight all the factors before you can make that decision.

The Solution

For a moment let us assume your finances are in great shape and you are contemplating early retirement. Next, you must decide if you are psychologically ready to retire early. Here are some of the major psychological issues to consider before taking the plunge.

- Boredom is the number one complaint in retirement. If you did not have many interests outside your work life, you may find retirement a challenge. Regardless of your age, start to prepare for early retirement now. Plan how you will fill up your days.
- Lack of job stress is a benefit of retirement and many people happily give up the stresses associated with the job while others thrive on the

daily challenges working presents. If you thrive on challenges, then early retirement may not be right option for you. Consider semi-retirement. Work part-time or only a few months out of the year in a job you like but that is perhaps less stressful. This provides a great psychological transition into full retirement, as well as financial benefits.

- The loss of social interaction is another big complaint with retirees. If all your friends are work buddies, you may find it difficult to find new daytime friends who, like you, do not work Monday through Friday, 9 to 5.
- It is common that only one spouse retires early. The working spouse may expect the retired spouse to keep house, or may resent watching the spouse sleep in while he or she trudges off to work, which can cause friction. Talk it over carefully with your spouse, so you both agree on expectations, such as travel and housework, well in advance of the scheduled retirement date.
- In a bad economy, when people are being laid off, some take advantage of early retirement packages. While the package figures may look good at the time, before you accept an early retirement package make sure you are financially ready to accept full-time retirement.
- Money worries are a big issue if you are planning for early retirement. Unexpected expenses, an economic downturn and inflation can eat away at a retirement nest egg. The worry can be especially bad for early retirees who have to make their money last 10 to 15 years longer.

Planning for early retirement is a two step process:

1) You must be sure you have saved and invested enough money to last you, in some cases, two times longer than if you retired at your full retirement age.
2) You must also be psychologically prepared for a big change, not only in your daily routine, but in your spending habits as well.

Balancing your financial and emotional needs will help you prepare for a successful early retirement.

The Resources

www.retireearlyhomepage.com/

An online magazine for people who are retired.

http://fireseeker.com/

A free calculator to help you determine how long your money will last.

34

Post-Retirement
Planning

The Challenge

The argument that retirees need less money during retirement than during their working years may not be correct. While in theory it should be true, there are several reasons why it is not as true today as it might have been a decade or two ago.

- Today, more than 30 percent of homeowners 65 and older still carry a mortgage balance of $30,000 or more. The monthly payments, although tending to be lower, can still eat up a significant portion of a retiree's fixed monthly income.
- Adult children who are having trouble landing a job, are out of a job or are going through a divorce are moving back in with the folks (sometimes with their own families in tow). A phrase coined in the UK sums up this new trend rather nicely–KIPPERS (Kids In Parents' Pockets Eroding Retirement Savings). In Japan, kids living at home are called Parasite Singles. In the U.S. they are often referred to Boomerangers (as in they keep returning).
- Healthcare costs are rising rapidly and now take up to 20 percent of the average retiree's income and show no signs of slowing down anytime soon.

Many retirees report that some expenses decreased after they retired, while others, such as health care costs, increased. In order to keep up with increased costs, your investments must continue growing long after you have retired. You might be in retirement mode, but that is not the state you want your investments to be in. In short, you can retire from working but you can never retire from working your investments.

The Facts

When you retire, your spending pattern may change. Some changes may occur gradually, with aging. For example:

- Health care expenditures tend to increase with age at all income levels.
- Household utilities tend to decrease with age at lower income levels and

increase with age at higher income levels (fewer occupants in the residence).

- Household operations tend to increase with age at all income levels.
- Mortgage, rent and repair expenditures tend to decrease with age at all income levels.
- Entertainment expenditures tend to increase with age at lower income levels and decrease with age at higher income levels (attend more movies).
- Educational expenditures tend to decrease with age at all income levels.

Other changes in expenditures occur directly related to a change in employment. For example:

- Food expenditures tend to decrease upon retirement for lower income levels and increase for higher income levels (more entertainment and restaurant meals).
- Apparel expenditures tend to decrease upon retirement at all income levels.

Guestimating your expenses after you retire is just that, a guess. There are some expenses, such as mortgage and utilities, you can count on remaining somewhat constant while others, such as taxes, health care and insurance, are less predictable over time.

The Solution

One of the biggest mistakes retirees make is overspending their retirement savings the first few years of retirement. After all the years of toiling and saving, it may seem liberating to finally take your dream vacation, purchase the boat you have always wanted or buy a new car. The problem is most people do not realize that big purchases will have a negative effect on future earning power. If you have dipped into your retirement money to purchase a big-ticket item, you could be effectively reducing your income by 2 or more years. Knowing how much you will have and how much you can take out each year will help preserve your retirement savings.

When you retire there are five things you should do to make sure you have enough money put away to last your lifetime:

1. Analyze your investment portfolio results.

   Each year review your investment returns. If an investment is not performing as expected, move the money to another investment vehicle that is producing better returns. Review Chapter 10: *Your Investoment—ROI, ROA, ROE* to calculate your return on investment.

2. Calculate your semi-annual expenses.

   Figure out how much you will need each year for living expenses and to maintain your lifestyle. If your living expenses are higher than your earnings, look for ways to reduce your expenses.

3. Draw up a budget breakdown.

Divide your budget into groups to determine where you are spending the majority of your money and find ways to reduce the expense.

4. Tie up excess funds.

To resist the temptation to spend more than your budget allows, keep only the amount of living expenses you will need each month in your checking account and place all other extra cash into a money market account. If your money is not easily accessible, you will not be so quick to tap into it.

5. Conduct a retirement income replacement ratio review.

Include all monthly or semi-annual costs and expenses. A comprehensive retirement income replacement ratio study requires you to determine:
 • your post-retirement income, including:
  – Social Security;
  – earned income from working beyond retirement;
  – personal savings; and
  – private pension plans (personal and employer provided qualified and non-qualified plans).
 • offsets resulting from:
  – Federal, state and local tax rates;
  – various levels of taxation on Social Security benefits;
  – offsets in Social Security benefits by post-retirement earned income; and
  – factors that cause changes in spending patterns post-retirement.

Your retirement income replacement ratio is the percentage of working income that you need to maintain the same lifestyle you enjoyed before retirement, which usually is 60 percent to 90 percent of your pre-retirement costs. You can determine your retirement income replacement ratio using this formula:

1) Gross final pre-retirement income - pre-retirement taxes = disposable income.
 ($60,000 - 16,800 = $43,200 disposable income)
2) Disposable income - pre-retirement savings yearly distribution amount = spendable income.
 ($43,200 - $32,000 = $11,200 in spendable income)
3) Spendable income + post-retirement expenditure change = expected after-tax retirement income.
 ($11,200 + $10,000 = $22,200 expected after-tax retirement income)
4) After-tax retirement income + post-retirement taxes = post-retirement income needed. Your post-retirement taxes may decrease to the 17 percent bracket.
 ($22,200 + $3,440 = $25,640 post-retirement income needed)
5) Post-retirement income expected/gross pre-retirement income (item 1) = income replacement ratio.
 ($25,640/$60,000 = .43 or 43 percent as your income replacement ratio)

To determine if you have enough money saved for retirement, calculate your own retirement income replacement ratio and create a plan for your retirement spending that is consistent with your allocation of investments and required minimum distributions to ensure your money will last your entire lifetime.

When estimating your future costs, keep in mind that at some point during your lifetime you may need to cover full-time nursing or hospitalization costs. These types of costs can run quite high, between $5,000-$8,000 a month, and can quickly eat up any savings you have. To offset these costs, long-term and health care insurance can significantly defray these costs. See Chapter 41: *The Insurance Game–Health & Disability*, and Chapter 42: *Long-Term Health Care Insurance* for more information.

The Resources

www.tcalc.com/tvwww.dll?Spend?Cstm=intuit3&IsAdv=1

> This calculator can be used to find out how much you can withdraw from an account over a period of time and how much you must have in initial savings.

www.investopedia.com/articles/retirement/06/RethinkNeeds.asp

> An excellent article that helps those approaching retirement think about their needs versus their wants.

www.activeretriement.com

> Guides, investment strategies and retirement statistics.

http://info.ag.uidaho.edu/Resources/PDFs/CIS1013.pdf

> This worksheet will help you determine your post-retirement expenses.

35

Filing for
Social Security Benefits

The Challenge

The Social Security Act was signed into law in 1935 as a means to provide economic security to old-age individuals.

...The Social Security Act offers to all our citizens a workable and working method of meeting urgent present needs and of forestalling future needs... We can never insure 100 percent of the population against 100 percent of the hazards and vicissitudes of life, but we have tried to frame a law which will give some measure of protection to the average citizen and to his family against the loss of a job and against poverty-ridden old age.

–President Franklin Roosevelt

Meeting the needs of the time, Social Security was created to supplement an existing pension, retirement savings or investment dividends program. It was never designed to replace a worker's full income upon retirement. More than 60 years later, Social Security continues to provide a steady income to millions of retirees who might not have any other savings or retirement programs to draw from.

When is the right time to file for Social Security benefits? Each year you receive a Social Security Statement showing your Social Security earnings history and how much Social Security taxes you have paid into the program. It also estimates your future benefits and tells you how to qualify for those benefits. The Social Security Statement is a free service of the Social Security Administration. This will give you a good estimate of how much you will collect if you file early retirement or at full retirement age. When you file is a personal decision.

The Social Security Administration suggests that an individual should apply for social security benefits 3 months before his or her planned retirement date.

* You can apply for Social Security benefits if you are 61 years and 9 months old to begin receiving early retirement or spouse's benefits within 4 months.

- You can apply for Social Security benefits three months before your full retirement age to begin receiving retirement or spouse's benefits within 4 months.
- You can apply for Medicare benefits if you are 64 years and 9 months old to begin receiving Medicare coverage at age 65.

Even if you do not plan to start your benefits before age 65, you should still register with the Social Security Administration because you are eligible for Medicare benefits beginning at age 65. You do not have to receive Social Security benefits to qualify for Medicare benefits.

The Facts

When you apply for benefits, you will need to provide the following information on your application:

- Your or your spouse's Social Security number.
- Your W-2 forms or self-employment tax return for last year.
- The name and address of each employer for the last 2 years.
- Military discharge papers if you were in the U.S. military between 1939 and 1968, or the beginning and ending dates of each period of active duty service.
- Date of birth of your current spouse and any former spouse(s), plus marriage and divorce information.
- Names of unmarried children (your dependent natural children, adopted children, stepchildren and possibly your dependent grandchildren and step grandchildren who live with you) under age 18, or age 18 and still attending secondary school (below college level on a full-time basis), or any child disabled before age 22.
- Proof of U.S. citizenship or lawful alien status if you (or a spouse or child is applying for benefits) were not born in the U.S.
- The name of your bank and your account number so your benefits can be directly deposited into your account.
- Your Social Security Statement. Review the list of yearly earnings carefully using your own records to make sure the information is correct for each year you worked, especially years after 1977 and any years you served on active duty in the U.S. military. You are the only person who can look at the earnings chart and know whether or not it is complete.

Social Security benefits are paid each month. Generally, the day of the month you receive your benefit payment depends on the birth date of the person on whose earnings record you receive benefits. For example, if you get benefits as a retired worker, your benefit will be determined by your birth date. If you receive benefits based on your spouse's work, your benefit payment date will be determined by your spouse's birth date.

Date of Birth	Benefits Paid Each Month on:
1st – 10th	Second Wednesday
11th – 20th	Third Wednesday
21st – 31st	Fourth Wednesday

Direct deposit is the recommended method of depositing retirement checks. It is a simple, safe and secure way to receive your benefits. Contact your bank to help you sign up. You also can sign up for direct deposit by contacting the Social Security Administration. If you do not have an account, you may want to consider an electronic transfer account (ETA). It is a low-cost account for recipients of federal payments. This low-cost federally insured account lets you enjoy the safety, security and convenience of automatic payments. To find an electronic transfer provider, visit *www.eta-find.gov*.

The Solution

You can apply for retirement benefits either in person or online.

To apply online, connect to the Social Security Benefit application at *www.ssa.gov/ applyforbenefits* and follow the instructions. Applying for benefits online offers several advantages, among them:

- You apply in the privacy of your own home, at your own pace.
- You avoid trips to a Social Security office, saving time and money.
- Your online application costs the U.S. taxpayer less to process.
- Your information is secure and kept private.

You can also apply by calling the toll-free number, 1.800.772.1213. Representatives can make an appointment for your application to be taken over the telephone or at any convenient Social Security office. People who are deaf or hard of hearing may call the toll-free TTY number, 1.800.325.0778.

If you have access to a computer with a secure Internet connection, just follow three simple steps:

1. Go to the Social Security Website at *www.socialsecurity.gov* and click on Apply for Retirement Benefits.
2. Fill in the answers to the application questions on your computer screen and select the Sign Now button to send the application.

You can stop and save the information you already entered up to that point and finish the application on a different day if you need to. When you are ready to finish applying, select Restart Your Incomplete Application from the menu, then enter your Social Security number and the confirmation number given to you. Your application is not final until you fill in the last page on the application screen and select the Sign Now button to submit your application to the Social Security Administration.

Once you have completed the online application you will also need to submit original documents or copies to be certified by the issuing office. You can mail or bring them into a Social Security office. You will need to provide the following originals after you apply online:

- Birth certificate or other proof of birth.
- Naturalization papers.
- U.S. military discharge paper(s).
- W-2 form(s) and/or self-employment tax returns for last year.

Photocopies of W-2 forms, self-employment tax returns or medical documents are acceptable but you must provide the originals of most other documents, such as your birth certificate. All documents you supply will be returned to you.

If you do not have a birth certificate, you may request one from the state where you were born. See below in The Resources section for where to write for vital records for details on where to write in your state.

If you wish, a representative can help you when you do business with Social Security or fill out the application online. For more information about your right to representation, view *Your Right to Representation Publication #10075* or view it online at *www.socialsecurity.gov/pubs/10075.html* .

If you choose to have a representative help you complete the process, he or she must complete *Form SSA-1696-U4 (Appointment of Representative)*. To obtain a copy of this form, as well as a comprehensive explanation of the representative process, visit *www.socialsecurity.gov/representation*. If the claimant appoints a representative, the representative cannot charge or collect a fee for those services without first getting written approval from the Social Security Administration, even if the claim is denied. To get this approval, the representative must use one of Social Security's fee authorization processes. To learn more, visit *www.socialsecurity.gov/representation/overview.htm*.

The Resources

www.cdc.gov/nchs/howto/w2welcome.htm

For information on where to write for vital records in your state.

www.ssa.gov/mystatement/

To learn more about your Social Security Statement.

www.socialsecurity.gov/representation/overview.htm

For an overview of representative fees.

36

Working & Collecting Social Security

The Challenge

Is it beneficial to continue working into retirement while still collecting full benefits? For many, retirement does not signal the end of working, but a career and lifestyle transition filled with many options—perhaps continuing to work (although at a different pace), returning to school for additional training or education or attending Elderhostels around the world, becoming more involved in volunteer work, or simply enjoying leisure and travel possibilities. It may also signal an opportunity to change careers or venture into entrepreneurship.

Yet for some older workers, retirement of any sort is not an option because of financial necessity. Whether stuck in low-paying jobs with little or no retirement plans or through poor planning or other financial hardships, these seniors need jobs just to survive.

But why should you work or volunteer if you do not have to? Experts suggest working helps older folks keep their minds and bodies active, provides social interaction and relationships, supports their value system and work ethic, adds meaning to life, fights stereotypes that only the young are good workers, provides contact with other individuals and produces a sense of identity, worth and a reason to keep active.

The Facts

Some retirees are unaware that they can continue working full or part-time and still collect full retirement benefits. There are, however, specific guidelines you must follow or your benefits may be reduced.

A few simple facts:

- If you have reached full retirement age and continue working, you may keep all of your benefits, no matter how much you earn. The key is reaching the full retirement age as determined by the Social Security Administration.

- If you retired early (before your designated full retirement age), your benefits will be reduced based on the amount you earned during the year.
- If you return to work after you start receiving full benefits, your income may be applied to your overall earnings calculation and you may receive a higher benefit based on your current earnings.
- If you delay collecting on your Social Security benefits until age 70½, your total monthly benefit may increase up to 24 percent. See Chapter 35: *Filing for Benefits*.

If you work for someone else, only your wages count toward Social Security's earnings limits. If you work for wages, income counts when it is earned, not when it is paid. If you have income that you earned in one year, but the payment was made in the following year, it should not be counted as earnings for the year you receive it. Some examples are accumulated sick or vacation pay and bonuses. Some companies allow employees to apply accumulated sick or vacation pay towards their earnings to help bolster their last year's income. Be aware, however, that any accumulated pay will be taxed at a higher rate and if you participate in a retirement plan, a portion of the payout will be deposited into your retirement account, usually pretax, which will reduce your taxable earnings and result in a smaller lump sum payout than you may be expecting.

If you are self-employed, income only counts when you receive it–not when you earn it–unless it is paid in a year after you become entitled to Social Security and earned before you became entitled. The Social Security Administration (SSA) counts only your net earnings from self-employment. Income earned from other sources, such as other government benefits, investment earnings, interest, pensions, annuities and capital gains, are not counted.

Also, if you are self-employed the rules about how much you can work are different than if you worked for someone else. The SSA considers how much work you do in your business to determine whether you are fully- or semi-retired. One way your status is determined is by looking at the amount of time that you spend working. In general, if you work more than 45 hours a month in self-employment, you are not retired; if you work less than 15 hours a month, you are retired. If you work between 15 and 45 hours a month, you will not be considered retired if it is in a job that requires a lot of skill or you are managing a sizable business.

The Solution

Receiving Benefits While Working

If you have reached full retirement age and continue working, you may keep all of your benefits, no matter how much you earn. There are no rules limiting your annual income, unless of course, you are self-employed or the owner of a business.

If you are younger than the required full retirement age in the year you retire, Social Security will deduct $1 from your benefits for each $2 you earned above $12,000.

If you turn your full retirement age during any part of a full year, Social Security will deduct $1 from your benefits for each $3 you earned above $31,800 until the month you turned your full retirement age.

For example, you begin receiving Social Security benefits at age 62 in January 2005 and your payment is $600 per month ($7,200 for the year). During the year, you work and earn $20,000 ($8,000 above the $12,000 limit). Social Security would withhold $4,000 of your Social Security benefits ($1 for every $2 you earn over the limit), but you would still receive $3,200 in benefits.

Again, imagine you were below full retirement age at the beginning of the year, but reach full retirement age in August. You earned $33,000 in the 7 months from January through July. During this period, Social Security would withhold $400 ($1 for every $3 you earned above the $31,800 limit). You would still receive $3,800 of your Social Security benefits. And, starting in August (when you reach full retirement age), you would begin receiving your full benefits, no matter how much you earn.

Sometimes people who retire in mid-year already have earned more than the yearly earnings limit. That is why there are special rules that apply to earnings for 1 year, usually the first year of retirement. Under these rules, you can get a full Social Security check for any whole month you are retired, regardless of your yearly earnings.

If you return to work after you start receiving full retirement age benefits you may be able to receive a higher benefit based on those earnings. This is because Social Security automatically re-computes your benefit amount after the additional earnings are credited to your earnings record. Your original Social Security benefit was based on your highest years of earnings. Each year, the Social Security Administration reviews the records for all Social Security recipients who work. If your latest year of earnings turns out to be one of your highest years, your benefits are refigured and you are paid any increase due. This is an automatic process and is usually completed by October of the following year. For example, by October 2007, you should get an increase for your 2006 earnings if those earnings raised your benefit. The increase would be retroactive to January 2007.

If you continue to work, should you continue to save? It is always smart planning to continue saving even if you are working during retirement. However, if you continue to work and you are over age 70½, you should be aware of certain restrictions:

- You can continue to contribute to a Roth IRA and to your company-sponsored plan, but not a traditional IRA.
- You must begin to take distributions from your traditional IRA or your company-sponsored plan now or face penalties. If you take the distribution, you may roll that distribution into a Roth account. When you take a distribution you will be required to pay taxes on the interest earned, but there is nothing preventing you from depositing that money into a Roth account to continue funding your retirement savings.
- You are never required to take distributions from a Roth IRA.

The Resources

Visit the following Websites for more information on social security benefits and working beyond retirement age:

www.aarp.org

AARP retirement resources and advice.

www.ssa.gov

Social Security Administration.

www.quintcareers.com

Working beyond retirement Website.

www.retiredbrains.com

Helping seniors find jobs.

www.careerbuilder.com

Careerbuilder online national job database.

www.socialsecurity.gov/retire2/whileworking.htm

Working-while-retired calculator

www.socialsecurity.gov/OACT/COLA/RTeffect.html

Earnings test calculator lets you see how your earnings could affect your benefit payments.

www.socialsecurity.gov/pubs/ageincrase.htm

Determine your full retirement age.

37

Retirement
Withdrawal Rules

The Challenge

Age 70½ is a milestone age. That is the year the IRS requires you to take your first distribution called required minimum distribution (RMD) from your retirement account, even if you are still working. The reason? The IRS does not want you to leave too much tax-free money to your heirs, and this requirement forces you to begin taking withdrawals from your retirement nest eggs each year or pay a big penalty. This RMD must come out of tax-deferred retirement savings accounts. This includes several popular IRAs–traditional, simplified employee pension, or SEP, and SIMPLE accounts–as well as certain employer-sponsored plans.

Although you may be tempted to leave the account untouched if you do not need the money and do not want to pay taxes on unnecessary withdrawals, that is not a good idea. Failure to withdraw the required amount will trigger a hefty excess accumulation tax equal to 50 percent of the required distribution you did not take. For example, if you did not withdraw the required $1,000 from your traditional IRA, the tax charge is $500. For a taxpayer in the 25 percent income tax bracket, that is twice what you would have paid in taxes if you had followed the RMD rule.

The IRS may waive the penalty, but you must show that your distribution shortfall was due to a reasonable error and that you are taking steps to correct the situation. But to do so, you must file *Form 5329* (part VIII), pay the excess accumulation tax and attach a letter of explanation. If the IRS rules you should not be penalized, the excess tax you paid will be refunded.

The challenge is understanding required minimum distribution rules, determining how much you must take each year and what you can and cannot do with the money.

The Facts

Beginning at age 70½ you can no longer make contributions to certain retirement accounts and you must take your first minimum withdrawal no later than April 1st or face penalties. One consequence of taking distributions from your IRA also means you pay tax on the income. If you fail to take at least the minimum withdrawal amount each year, you will owe a 50 percent penalty on the shortfall. Of course, you can always take out more than the minimum and pay the additional income taxes on the lump sum.

Keep in mind that the IRA minimum distribution rules apply to traditional IRAs and Simplified Employee Pension (SEP) accounts, as well as Simple-IRAs, since they all are considered IRAs for this purpose. Roth IRA owners, however, are exempt from the minimum withdrawal rules as long as the original account owner is alive, since the amount invested into a Roth account was already taxed when it was deposited and is therefore not tax-deferred.

You can take your first minimum withdrawal during the year you turn 70½, or you can take it by April 1 of the year after you turn 70½. Then for each subsequent year, you must take at least the required minimum withdrawal by Dec. 31 of that year. When you take your distribution can have significant tax implications. After all, if you do not take your initial minimum withdrawal during the year you turn 70½, you will need to take two withdrawals and pay the resulting double dip of taxes in the following year.

The amount of each minimum withdrawal depends on your IRA account balance at the end of the previous year divided by a joint life-expectancy figure for you and your account beneficiary. The younger you are, the longer your life expectancy figure and, consequently, the lower your required minimum withdrawal.

The IRS has created three tables based on life expectancies to figure the minimum withdrawal amount:

1. Retirement plan beneficiaries (other than spouses).
2. Married account owners with spouses more than 10 years younger.
3. The uniform lifetime table for single and married savers with spouses closer to their own ages.

To calculate the year's minimum distribution amount, take the age of the retiree and find the corresponding distribution period. Then divide the value of the IRA by the distribution period to find the required minimum distribution. To simplify the calculation use used the table designation (married with a spouse more than 10 years younger) for an IRA account amount of $100,000 less the previous year's distribution amount (assuming no interest is earned).

Age of Retiree	Joint Life Expectancy	Account Balance	Required Distribution Amount
70	27.4	$100,000	$3,649
71	26.5	$96,351	$3,635
72	25.6	$92,716	$3,753
73	24.7	$88,963	$3,738
74	23.8	$85,225	$3,722
75	22.9	$81,503	$3,705
76	22.0	$81,466	$3,843
77	21.2	$77,623	$3,824
78	20.3	$73,799	$3,785
79	19.5	$70,014	$3,744
80	18.7	$66,270	$3,702
81	17.9	$62,568	$3,659
82	17.1	$58,909	$3,614
83	16.3	$55,295	$3,567
84	15.5	$51,728	$3,495
85	14.8	$48,233	And so on up to 115 yrs. of age

This table also can be used to determine the minimum distributions required from qualified company retirement plans, such as 401(k)s and profit-sharing plans. Again, Roth IRAs are not affected by the new rules, because these accounts do not have required minimum distribution amounts.

The Solution

When you turn age 70½ you must take your RMD. You have two choices: you can take the required minimum distribution as allowed by the IRS or you can take the entire lump sum. In either event, you will be taxed on whichever amount you take.

There are other important factors to consider:

• The minimum withdrawal rules automatically assume you have designated a person 10 years your junior as your IRA beneficiary. It does not make any difference to the IRS if your actual designated beneficiary is older than the 10-year age bracket. The only exception to the 10 years younger beneficiary rule is when your spouse is designated as the sole IRA beneficiary and he or she is more than 10 years younger. In this somewhat unusual circumstance, you are allowed to calculate your IRA minimum withdrawals using more favorable joint life-expectancy figures based on the actual ages of you and your spouse. How these rules will affect you depends on your age and how much money you have in your IRA.

- Married account owners with spouses more than 10 years younger use a different life expectancy table to determine how much must be withdrawn each year. Since its calculations incorporates the younger age of the spouse and spread withdrawals over a longer life expectancy, these account owners do not have to take out as much and can leave more in the account to earn more income. Refer to IRS *Publication 590* to find your divisor, which will be based on your age and your spouse's age. The IRS continues to make revisions to life expectancy tables to reflect today's longer life spans. Under the new distribution guidelines, an individual with sufficient income from other sources can withdraw less from a retirement account, letting it grow for a while longer.

It is important for you to understand and adhere to IRS RMD regulations to avoid paying stiff penalties.

When you take your RMD there are specific rules with what you can and cannot do with the money, such as purchase life insurance or invest in collectibles or stocks. Consult with your financial advisor before investing.

The Resources

www.irs.gov/publications/p590/ch01.html#d0e5724

Required Minimum Distributions, IRS *Publication 590*.

www.bankrate.com/brm/itax/tips/20030325a1.asp?caret=14

Bankrate.com article about withdrawing from your IRA.

38

IRA
Special Withdrawal
Allowances

The Challenge

Perhaps your retirement plan is on track and you have diligently put money into your accounts every year. Suddenly, out of the blue, you find yourself in a financial jam. You may have lost your job or racked up a large sum of medical bills or the student loan did not go through as planned and tuition is now due. You need cash, fast. All that money you have so carefully put away is needed now. It seems a shame that it is just sitting there, collecting interest and cannot be accessed for more immediate needs.

Take heart, the IRS is not completely inflexible. There is a way you can take money out of an individual retirement plan without being hit with a penalty and paying additional taxes, but there are stipulations on how you money can be used.

The Facts

When you take money out of an individual retirement account before you reach age 59½, the Internal Revenue Service considers it a premature distribution. In addition to owing any tax that might be due on the money, you will also face a 10 percent penalty charge on the amount.

There are however, specific life events when the IRS says it is okay to use your retirement savings early–to help purchase your first home or pay higher-education expenses.

The IRS will not assess an early withdrawal penalty if your IRA money is applied to qualified schooling costs for yourself, your spouse, your children or your grandchildren. Funding higher education costs for any other family members, including nieces, aunts, grandparents, etc., does not qualify and you will be taxed and penalized for the early withdrawal.

Higher Education

The eligible student must attend an IRS-approved institution. This is usually any college, university, vocational school or other post-secondary facility that meets federal student aid program requirements. The school can be public, private or non-profit as long as it is accredited. Once enrolled, you can use retirement money to pay tuition and fees and buy books, supplies and other required equipment. Expenses for special-needs students also count. And if the student is enrolled at least half-time, room and board also meet IRS expense guidelines.

First-Time Home Buyer

You can use up to $10,000 in IRA funds toward the purchase of your first home. If you are married and you and your spouse are both first-time buyers, you each can pull from retirement accounts to create a combined $20,000 in residential cash. The IRS's definition of a first-time homebuyer is rather broad. Technically, you do not have to be purchasing your very first house to be considered a first-time buyer. You qualify if you and your spouse did not own a principal residence at any time during the previous 2 years. You can also use your IRA funds for a down payment for you, your spouse, a child, grandchild or parent.

It is very important to plan carefully when to withdraw your money. Timing is everything. If you take the money out too soon, the IRS may disqualify the withdrawal. You must use the IRA funds within 120 days of withdrawal to pay qualified acquisition costs. This may include the costs of buying, building and rebuilding, as well as any settlement, financing or closing costs.

These home-buying IRA options apply to traditional retirement accounts. The rules are a bit different if your nest egg is in a Roth IRA. In order to withdraw funds early from a Roth IRA without penalty, you must meet the time limit requirement. The $10,000 you take out for your first home is a qualified distribution as long as you have had your Roth account for 5 years. After 5 years you can take out your retirement money without any penalty.

If, however, you have had your Roth IRA account for less than 5 years, the withdrawal is considered an early distribution. This may be true for many people since Roth accounts were not created until 1998. As with a traditional IRA early withdrawal, a Roth holder can use the first-home exception to avoid the 10 percent penalty, but may still owe tax on earnings withdrawn.

Check with your financial planner or IRS *Publication 590, Individual Retirement Arrangements* regarding specific rules about the order in which you can take unqualified Roth distributions. You can reduce your tax liability by first withdrawing already taxed contributions you made to your Roth. There are several rules about contributions, converting and rolling over traditional IRAs and earnings to Roth accounts.

Other circumstances that allow you to take distributions without penalty include:

- Payment of excessive medical expenses in excess of 7.5 percent of your adjusted gross income and not covered by an insurance policy.
- Payment of medical insurance premiums while unemployed.
- Total and permanent disability costs and expenses.
- Distribution of account assets to a beneficiary after you die; and
- Long-term disability.

Additionally, if you live or lived in the Hurricane Katrina zone, you could qualify for a new exception to the withdrawal rule. You can withdraw, after August 25, 2005 and before January 1, 2007, up to $100,000 from any IRA without penalty as long as the funds are used to rebuild your home. Withdrawals are still subject to any applicable income taxes, but the 10 percent penalty will be waived on any amount less than $100,000.

Finally, if you want to retire early or if you are in serious financial straits and need to tap into your IRA money there is a way to do it without triggering a penalty: Take the money out in substantially equal payments over your lifetime. IRS rules require that you take at least one payment annually for the exception to apply. Actuarial tables are used to determine life expectancy and, in essence, you are turning your retirement plan into an annuity (also called an annuity distribution), or annuitizing an IRA. Again, the key is to take payouts on a specific schedule. This method allows you to begin withdrawing from your IRA early as long as the amounts are determined by an IRS calculated life-expectancy table (see Chapter 37: *Retirement Withdrawal Rules*).

Taking an early withdrawal is not popular or necessarily a good idea, as illustrated through this example.

If you have $100,00 in an IRA account and you decided to take distribution payments early—say age 35—you would have to take $2,500 a year for 40 years. This severely limits the ability for this money to grow. If for any reason you decided taking the distribution was a bad decision and try to reduce the payment to $2,000, the IRS will hit you with a 10 percent penalty. IRS rules state that you cannot change the payment plan for 5 years or until you reach age 59½, whichever is later.

But where it does make sense to take an annuity distribution payment on a retirement plan is if the owner of the IRA is in his or her 50s or early 60s and has lost his or her job or has become ill. If there is a substantial amount of money in the IRA, an annuity distribution can be set up as a one-life annuity or a two-life annuity for married couples. The estimated life expectancy of a one-life annuity on a 55 year old is 28.6 years. The life expectancy of a two-life annuity is 34.4 years. Simply put, the annual payment on a $500,000 IRA, paid out for the one-life annuity at equal payments for 28.6 years, would be approximately $17,483. The annual payment for the two-life annuity would be approximately $14,535.

To emphasize an important point again, early-withdrawal exceptions do not eliminate your tax bill if you take the money out of a traditional IRA. Contributions to IRAs are pre-tax, meaning taxes have not been deducted from your earning and that makes them tax-deferred investments. Taxes are paid when withdrawals begin. Roth accounts are funded with after-tax dollars, meaning taxes have already been deducted from your earnings. You are taxed on the interest earned only from Roth accounts. So when you take the money out of such an account, regardless of your age or the purpose of the withdrawal, you will owe your regular tax rate on the amount withdrawn.

You must inform the IRS that you used the retirement money early for a tax-acceptable purpose by filing IRS *Form 5329*. When you fill out the form you will also enter a code, found in the form's instructions. This form lets the IRS know the distribution is penalty free.

The Solution

Life may come at you hard sometimes. Having needed resources at your disposal to cover some of life's most difficult moments involves planning. Your retirement money should work for you, building a nest egg, allowing you to comfortably retire when it is time. Tapping into those resources will keep your retirement plan on track. You may lose some interest income when the funds are dispersed, but you also have the opportunity to repay your accounts when your situation improves. Consult with your financial advisor or company plan coordinator for borrowing and repayment details.

The Resources

www.moneycentral.msn.com/content/Taxes/P82396.asp

For information on how to tap into your nest egg penalty-free.

www.investopedia.com/articles/retirement/03/070203.asp

For an article on borrowing from your IRA.

Spousal Benefits

The Challenge

In previous chapters we have talked extensively about the importance of creating a retirement plan and then funding it on a regular basis. This chapter will discuss the importance of building a retirement nest egg for your spouse.

If your spouse is also working and earning income, he or she can establish his or her own retirement account. But what if you spouse is not working? One of the eligibility requirements for making a contribution to an IRA is that you must have taxable compensation. Here is where one of the benefits of marriage comes into play. For married couples that file a joint return, the working spouse is allowed to make a spousal IRA contribution to the IRA of the spouse who has no taxable compensation (know as the non-working spouse.)

Most married couples will tell you that the security of each spouse funding their own retirement plan is not only smart planning, but also reassuring. Therefore, helping to fund your spouse's retirement nest egg may be equally as important as funding your own, as retirement assets may be shared during your retirement years.

The Facts

Here are some surprising (or maybe not so surprising) facts:

- Of the 59 million wage and salaried women working in the United States as of February 2006, 53 percent do not have private pension coverage.
- Less than half of all workers participate in the company sponsored retirement plan. Thirty-two percent of the workforce has no savings set aside specifically for retirement.
- Women's employment patterns are different than men's. Women are more likely to work in part-time jobs, which often do not offer pension coverage, or may work fewer years in pension-covered employment because of interruptions in their careers to take care of family members.

- On average, a woman retiring at age 65 can expect to live another 18.6 years (to age 84.6), or almost 4 years longer than a male retiring at the same age (to age 80.3), which requires additional savings for these extra years.
- Studies indicate that women tend to invest more conservatively than men, receiving lower rates of return from their investment over time, thus reducing the amount of savings they have at retirement.

In order for a working spouse to make IRA contributions for a non-working spouse he or she must:

- Be married;
- file a joint income-tax return;
- have compensation or earned income of at least the amount you contribute to your IRAs; and
- be under age 70½ for the year in which the contribution is being made. However, there are no age limits that apply to Roth IRA contributions.

Just as there are limits on how much you can contribute in a tax year to your own IRA, there are limits on how much you can fund a spouse's IRA. The contribution limit that applies to you also applies to your spouse. For example, for tax year 2006, the contribution limit is $4,000. If you contribute to both your IRA and your spouses, you may contribute no more than $8,000 in total. However, if you are age 50 or older, there are special catch-up rules. Check with your financial advisor regarding the current rules.

Individual and IRA Maximum Contribution Limits

Tax Year	Individual Contribution Limit	Individual & Spousal IRA Combined Contribution Limit
2006	$4,000	$8,000
2007	$4,000	$8,000
2008	$5,000	$10,000
2009	$5,000 plus potential cost of living increases.	$10,000 plus potential cost of living increases.

How much of the contribution you can deduct depends on whether you participate in other defined plans and your income amount. If you do not participate in another defined plan, such as an employer-sponsored plan or 401(k), you will be able to deduct the full amount of your spousal IRA contribution. If you are covered by an employer-sponsored plan, your ability to deduct your spousal IRA contribution depends on your income and your tax filing status.

Social Security provides spousal benefits as well. A quick overview of what you can anticipate from current Social Security benefits is as follows:

- Couples are not penalized if they are married. Lifetime earnings are calculated for each individual independently to determine their Social Security benefit amount and will not be reduced due to marriage.
- If you have been married for 10 years and then divorce, you will receive benefits under the same circumstances as a current spouse. Benefits paid to you, as the surviving divorced spouse, will not affect the benefit rates for other beneficiaries. You cannot receive benefits if you remarry before the age of 60 (50 if disabled), unless the latter marriage ends, whether by death, divorce or annulment. However, if you remarry after age 60 (50 if disabled), you may still receive payments based on your former spouse's record.
- You can still draw benefits even if you never worked and did not earn the required credits to draw benefits. At full retirement age you can apply to receive a benefit equal to one-half of your spouse's full retirement amount.
- A spouse may receive one-half of the retired worker's full benefit unless the spouse begins collecting benefits before full retirement age. In that case, the amount of the spouse's benefit is permanently reduced by a percentage based on the number of months before he or she reaches full retirement age.

For example, based on the full retirement age of 65, if a spouse begins collecting benefits:

- At 64, the benefit amount would be about 46 percent of the retired worker's full benefit.
- At age 63, the benefit amount would be about 42 percent.
- At age 62, the benefit amount would be about 37.5 percent.
- If you are eligible for both your own retirement benefit and for benefits as a spouse, Social Security will always pay your own benefit first. If your benefit as a spouse is higher than your retirement benefit, you will receive a combination of benefits equaling the higher spouse's benefit.

The Solution

You cannot depend on Social Security to provide fully for your spouse in the event of your death. You need to create other investment options to make up for any shortfalls in income that may exist. You should research investment plan options for your spouse with the same care you do for yourself. Here are some tips to consider as you develop a workable plan.

- Be aware of which plans allow you to deduct your contributions. Is the entire contribution tax deductible and deducted from your taxes? If the contributions are not deductible, would a Roth IRA be a better investment option? If so, then consider your contribution eligibility to a Roth IRA. If you are able to deduct your spouse's traditional IRA contribution but not your traditional IRA contribution, then it may be a better strategy to contribute to a Roth IRA for yourself instead.

- Understand the survivor benefits associated with each investment plan. One retirement plan may provide surviving spouses a lump-sum benefit, while another may pay a monthly or annuity form of payment. Before investing, read and understand any waiver or consent forms for your spouse's retirement plan distributions.

- IRAs must be held separately. The IRA you establish for your spouse must be in his or her name and with his or her tax identification number. Any IRA you establish for yourself must be established in your name and with your tax identification number.

- As part of the entire retirement package, consider purchasing life insurance to protect your spouse's retirement plan, as discussed in the Chapter 43: *Life Insurance*.

- You can designate anyone as the beneficiary of your retirement account. If, however, you participate in a qualified plan or live in a community property state, you must designate your spouse as the solo primary beneficiary of your plan. If you wish to designate someone else as beneficiary, your spouse must agree, in writing, that someone else will receive death benefits from your retirement account.

Creating a retirement plan for your spouse is as important as building a retirement plan for yourself. Take time to discuss investment options with a certified financial planner to create a realistic plan that you can start and build upon.

The Resources

www.investopedia.com/articles/retirement/

Investopedia.com provides numerous financial articles.

www.ssa.gov

Social Security Adminstration.

Sharing Benefits
with the Ex

The Challenge

A divorce can affect your financial position, especially if you are a woman over the age of 50 and have spent much of your married adult life raising the kids, managing the household and supporting your spouse and his career. For unmarried women—including widows—age 65 and older, Social Security comprises 52 percent of their total income. In contrast, Social Security benefits comprise only 38 percent of unmarried elderly men's retirement income and only 35 percent of elderly couples' income.

- Women reaching age 65 in 2004 are expected to live, on average, an additional 20 years compared with 17 years for men.
- Women represent 58 percent of all Social Security beneficiaries age 62 and older and approximately 70 percent of beneficiaries age 85 and older.
- The median earnings of full-time women workers in 2002 were $30,203, compared to $39,429 for men. Women's earnings relative to men have increased from 61 percent of men's earnings in the 1960s to 77 percent in 2002.
- Social Security provides dependent benefits to spouses, divorced spouses, elderly widows and widows with young children.

According to the Social Security Administration, the average monthly benefit paid in 2003—to a woman was $798, while the average benefit paid to a man was $1,039. Women's benefits average about 30 percent less then men's because they tend to be out of the workforce for longer periods of time to raise a family or care for an aging parent. Then, too, women still earn less than men in most industries. The less you earn, the lower your Social Security benefit is, since it is calculated on your earnings.

These statistics may seem bleak, but take heart. Even if you never worked as a wage earner outside the home you still earn the right to collect on your ex-spouses retirement benefits when you reach your full retirement age. The same rules apply to stay-at-home dads whose wife continued to work.

The Facts

Not many people realize they can collect social security benefits based on an ex-spouse's earnings when they both reach 62. However, you must qualify for such benefits.

If you have been married for at least 10 years, been divorced for at least 2 years and have not remarried, you can qualify for Social Security benefits based on your ex-spouse's earnings when you both reach age 62 and are eligible for benefits. That is the case even if your ex-spouse has remarried or has not retired and begun to receive benefits. You are entitled to receive 50 percent of your spouse's Social Security benefits as an ex-spouse. Keep in mind, though, that if you qualify for benefits based on your own employment history, you will receive the larger of the two payments. If you remarry someone who is receiving Social Security benefits as a dependent of a wage earner (such as a widower), your checks will continue. The rules say that your Social Security benefits based on your own work history must be less than half of your ex-spouse's benefits at age 65. So if you have had a spotty earnings record over the years or have worked in a low-paying field, you will be entitled to a larger benefit based on your spouse's work history than your own.

You can receive 50 percent of your ex's benefits while he or she is alive and 100 percent of your ex's benefits when he or she dies. If your ex-spouse remarries, you and his second spouse will both receive benefits.

Filing to collect the benefit will not harm your ex-spouse at all, nor will it reduce his or her payout. You ex will not be notified and will never know when you start receiving Social Security checks. In order to file without delay, you will need to know your ex-spouse's Social Security number.

If you are divorced (even if you have remarried), your ex-spouse may qualify for benefits on your record if you are 62 or older. In some situations, he or she may get benefits even if you are not receiving your benefits.

To qualify on your record, your ex-spouse must:

- Have been married to you for at least 10 years;
- be at least 62 years old;
- be unmarried; and
- not be eligible for an equal or higher benefit on his or her own Social Security record, or on someone else's Social Security record.

Again, the amount of benefits your divorced spouse gets has no effect on the amount of benefits you or your current spouse may receive.

Generally, benefits cannot continue to be paid if the divorced spouse remarries someone other than the former spouse, unless the latter marriage ends (whether by death, divorce or annulment) or the marriage is to a person entitled to certain types of Social Security auxiliary or survivor's benefits. A person can receive benefits as a surviving divorced spouse on the Social Security record of a former spouse who died fully insured, if he or she:

- Is at least age 60, or age 50 and disabled;
- was married to the former spouse for at least 10 years; and
- is not entitled to a higher Social Security benefit on his or her own record.

If the surviving divorced spouse age 60 or over applying for benefits remarried after age 60, or after age 50 and at the time of remarriage was entitled to disability benefits, the marriage is disregarded. If a person is already entitled to benefits as an aged or disabled surviving divorced spouse and remarries, benefits continue regardless of the person's age at the time of remarriage. The benefits paid to a divorced spouse or a surviving divorced spouse will not affect the benefit amount paid to other family members who receive benefits on the same record.

A person who is divorced after at least 10 years of marriage keeps certain benefit rights on his or her former spouse's record. In order to get benefits, the divorced spouse must be at least 62 years old and the former spouse must be eligible for benefits, but not necessarily receiving them. The maximum benefit is 50 percent of the benefit the worker would receive at full retirement age. However, benefits paid prior to full retirement age of the spouse are reduced based upon the age of the spouse at the time benefits are received.

Remarriage after age 60 (50 if disabled) will not prevent payments on a former spouse's record.

Social Security follows the rule that a divorced person married for 10 years or more is entitled to full spousal and survivor benefits, while one married less than 10 years is entitled to none. Some examples show how this rule affects benefits:

- If a spouse divorces a worker after 9 years, 11 months and 27 days of marriage, the spouse gets nothing from Social Security in auxiliary benefits and is entitled to no share of the worker's benefit. (Spouses can still get benefits on their own earnings records.)
- If a spouse divorces a worker after 40 years of marriage, the spouse is entitled to a spousal benefit of only one-half the benefit garnered by the worker as long as the worker is alive; however, should the worker die, the divorced spouse is entitled to a survivor's benefit equal to the worker's full benefit.
- If a single head of household raises children and works for 40 years at

$10,000 a year, he or she is entitled to substantially lower Social Security benefits than a spouse who never works and never raises children, as long as the non-working spouse was married to a rich worker for 10 years or more.

- A divorced person who was married to a much older worker will, on the average, get substantially more benefits than a divorced person who was married to a worker of the same age because those who marry older workers are more likely to get survivor's benefits, which are more generous than spousal benefits.
- A middle-class divorced spouse of a rich worker could face a significant marriage penalty forfeiting his or her survivor's benefits if he or she marries another middle-class worker.
- The amount of benefits a divorced spouse receives does not affect the amount of benefits another spouse receives on your ex-spouse's record.
- Many women get a higher benefit based on their ex-husband's work record than they get on their own record, especially if the ex-husband is deceased.

The Solution

If you have been through a divorce, it is to your advantage to familiarize yourself with Social Security benefits options. Take advantage of the resources available to you as you review your plans. Do your homework. If you meet all the required criteria, then applying for ex-spousal benefits may get you a higher benefit based on your ex-spouse's work record than your own record.

The Resources

www.ssa.gov/women and
www.nwlc.org/display.cfm?section=social%20security.

Both of these Websites provide more information on social security benefits as they apply to women.

The Insurance Game–
Health & Disability

The Challenge

Longevity also has its costs, with healthcare accounting for 20 percent of the average retiree's income according to the Health and Retirement Study, a study sponsored by the National Institute on Aging. That can add up to a significant expense that most people do not think about during their working years.

Consider these statistics: If you are age 65, married, ready to retire and have $200,000 available, you can probably pay for your medical costs in retirement. That is the latest estimate by Fidelity Investments based on the assumption there is no employer-provided retiree health coverage and taking into account your estimated life expectancy of an additional 17 or 20 years. The 2006 estimate includes expenses associated with Medicare Part B and D premiums, Medicare cost-sharing provisions–co-payments, coinsurance, deductibles and excluded benefits and prescription drug out-of-pocket costs. It does not include other health expenses, such as over-the-counter medications, most dental services and long-term care.

The number of companies offering retiree health benefits to employees continues to decline in double digit numbers each year according to the 2005 Kaiser Family Foundation and Health Research and Educational Trust, Employer Health Benefits Survey.

This, combined with health insurance premiums that are growing at a rate more than three times the growth of workers' earnings and two-and-a-half times the rate of consumer inflation, creates an unprecedented situation for individuals who may now need to account for more of their own health care costs in retirement.

The result is that health care costs could significantly erode your retirement savings if you do not plan for them. The challenge (and it really is a challenge) is to understand your health care options and to plan to receive the best benefits at the lowest cost.

The Facts

When you retire, your healthcare options may include Medicare Part A, B, and D or private retiree insurance often provided by your previous employer or a state-funded program.

Medicare is a health insurance program for:

- People age 65 or older;
- people under age 65 with certain disabilities; and
- people of all ages with End-Stage Renal Disease (permanent kidney failure requiring dialysis or a kidney transplant).

Medicare has:

- Part A Hospital Insurance
- Part B Medical Insurance
- Part D Prescription Plan

Today's Medicare offers more choices:

- The original Medicare Plan
- Medicare Advantage Plans
- Medicare Health Maintenance Organization (HMO) Plans
- Medicare Preferred Provider Organization (PPO) Plans
- Medicare Special Needs Plans
- Medicare Private Fee-for-Service (PFFS) Plans
- Other Medicare Health Plans (that are not Medicare Advantage Plans)
- Medicare Cost Plans
- Demonstrations
- PACE

Medicare Part A Hospital Insurance (HI) helps cover your inpatient care in hospitals, including critical access hospitals and skilled nursing facilities (not custodial or long-term care). It also helps cover hospice care and some home health care, although you must meet certain conditions to get these benefits. Most people do not have to pay a monthly payment, called a premium, for Part A. This is because you or your spouse paid Medicare taxes while working.

Medicare Part B Supplementary Medical Insurance (SMI) is voluntary and helps cover your doctors' services and outpatient care. It also covers some other medical services that Part A does not cover, such as some of the services of physical and occupational therapists and some home health care. Part B helps pay for these covered services and supplies when they are medically necessary. You pay the Medicare Part B premium each month ($88.50 per month in 2006). In some cases, this amount may be higher if you did not sign up for Part B when you first became eligible. If you do not take Part B when you are first eligible, the cost of Part B will go up 10 percent for each full 12-month period that you could have had Part B but did not sign up for it, except in special cases (employer or union coverage). You will have to pay this penalty as long as you have Part B. You also pay a Part B deductible each year before Medicare starts to pay its share. The Part B deductible for 2006 is $124. Medicare deductible and premium rates may change every year in January.

Medicare Part D Prescription Drugs started in May 2004 for individuals with income of $12,569 or less and for married couples with income of $16,862 or less. This is a prescription drug discount card program that shares the cost of drugs for low-income participants.

Medicare Advantage Plans are health plan options that are part of the Medicare Program. If you join one of these plans, you generally get all your Medicare-covered health care through that plan. This coverage can include prescription drug coverage. Medicare pays a set amount of money for your care every month to these private health plans whether or not you use services. In most of these plans, there generally are extra benefits and lower co-payments than in the Original Medicare Plan. However, you may have to see doctors that belong to the plan or go to certain hospitals to get services.

The Solution

Here are a few suggestions to reducing your medical costs when you retire:

- At the very least, factor into your retirement planning any future healthcare costs you might have to pay for. As mentioned above, health care costs are rising at almost 6 percent per year. Planning for these added costs now will help preserve your retirement savings when you retire.
- Consider setting up a separate healthcare account that you can tap into as needed for medical payments only. Make payments to this account annually to cover medical bills when you retire.
- Consider joining an association or membership group that may offer group insurance. Some trade associations may offer separate medical insurance at group rates or membership associations, such as AARP, may offer dental insurance coverage.
- Your employer may provide retiree healthcare benefits. Investigate and compare the policy coverage and costs to Medicare coverage before you sign up with your employer plan. Understand all the benefits Medicare and your retiree plan have to offer. Take special care to become knowledgeable with the rules and requirements of any plan. For example, you can be penalized with a higher premium if you do not sign up for Medicare Part B

when you apply for Medicare Part A. Not understanding the rules may cost you more.

- Make sure you take full advantage of available health resources. At age 65 you should sign up to receive Medicare benefits even if you do not file to receive Social Security benefits until age 70½.

Planning ahead will help preserve your retirement nest egg and ensure that you can make critical health decisions based on facts and necessity rather than finances alone.

The Resources

There is much more to Medicare than can possibly be included in this chapter. To understand all the benefits, visit the following resources:

- *www.seniorjournal.com/SeniorJournal.com*
- *www.kff.org*
  Talking About Medicare guide.
- *www.medicare.gov*
- *www.medicare.gov/MGCompare/Home.asp*
  Compare Medicare plan.

Get basic Medicare information by calling the National Medicare Hotline at 1-800-MEDICARE; TTY/TTD 1-877-486-2048.

Get information on Medicare enrollment and eligibility by calling the National Social Security Hotline at 1-800-772-1213.

You can also order *Medicare & You*, an overview of Medicare, by calling the hotline or by writing to Medicare Publications, Centers for Medicare and Medicaid Services, 7500 Security Blvd., Baltimore, MD 21244-1850.

Get referrals for local agencies that can help you obtain information and services in your community on home health care, nursing home care and long-term care insurance by calling the Eldercare Locator at 1-800-677-1116.

Request detailed information in English or Spanish about the Medicare Advantage (MA) plans available in your area by calling the automated Medicare Special Information number at 1-800-MEDICARE (1-800-633-4227).

Long-Term
Health Care Insurance

The Challenge

Consider this fact: 42 percent of Americans who are 65 today will enter a nursing home during their lifetimes. That is a huge increase over just a few decades ago. The current average annual cost of a 1-year nursing-home stay is more than $50,000. You would think that home health care would be much more reasonable, but it too averages more than $4,000 a month for part-time care. Women are especially vulnerable because they have a 50 percent greater likelihood of needing nursing-home care than men. Long-term health care is expensive and, as the average life expectancy of an average man is 80 and a woman is 84, the chances of needing long-term health care is great.

In years past, the elderly were cared for by family. Three (and sometimes four) generations were often living under the same roof, looking out for each other. Today's society does not always allow for such an arrangement, with dual income families, the older generation wanting more independence and families not living close to one another.

Whether you are married or single and with or without children, your total retirement planning should include the possibility you may be injured or require long-term care sometime during your lifetime.

The Facts

The premiums for long-term care insurance are not cheap, but unless you have assets of $2 million or more, you probably need it–especially if you want to preserve some assets for your children. Premiums vary based on your age, sex, geographical location and policy type, but annual costs can vary from $400 a year for a 40+ male to more than $3,000 for a man or woman aged 70 or older.

Long-term insurance is not an investment, it is insurance, and if you never use it you do not get your money back. But the chances of utilizing your long-term care insurance are 50-50. Long-term care insurance is a planning tool. You fund it and you hope that you will never need it. Consider it insurance to protect your portfolio of investments. For example, a 65-year old with a $300,000 portfolio could pay a hypothetical $1,000 to $2,000 in annual long-term care insurance premium, thereby protecting the overall portfolio from the potential of it being wiped out by future long-term care costs. If this person needed long-term care in 15 years, when costs are expected to exceed $100,000 per year, his or her portfolio would nearly be wiped out after the average 2.8 years of care (an estimated $280,000). Even a large portfolio of $1 million or more would lose almost 30 percent of its value without long-term care insurance. That is why those that buy long-term care insurance view it not as an investment, but as investment protection.

Consider these recent statistics:

- For a couple turning 65, there is a 70 percent chance that one of them will need long-term care.
- Over 50 percent of all people entering a care situation are penniless within 1 year.
- Ninety-seven percent of people over age 85 require assistance in the last year of life.
- Sixty percent of people over 75 need long-term care and many stay in facilities for about 3 years.
- By 2007, a private room will cost over $250/day ($94,000/year).
- Singles are at risk because they are usually not with someone who can properly care for them.

How much and what kind of coverage you want determines your annual premium. Below you will see the wide range of generalized premium expenses for a hypothetical person at several different ages. At the bottom of the page are some of the decisions that go into these types of premium calculations.

Entry Age	Generous Coverage	Minimal Coverage
40	$1,300/year	$ 55 / year
45	$1,400/year	$ 75 / year
50	$1,500/year	$ 80 / year
55	$1,700/year	$ 105 / year
60	$2,600/year	$ 150 / year
65	$3,400/year	$ 220 / year
70	$5,000/year	$ 355 / year
80	$7,900/year	$ 605 / year
85	$11,900/year	$ 1,065 / year

Every plan is different and you should review each plan carefully to compare benefits and coverage. As shown in the table, minimal coverage may cover only a portion of your daily costs. Generous coverage may cover three times more of the daily cost and incorporate home care benefits. Premium costs are hypothetical and do not represent any one particular long-term insurance provider.

Most people believe that Medicare will cover most health issues and that is correct as long as the health problem is short-term. Medicare is not designed to cover any long-term care. It does cover some limited convalescent skilled nursing care and some limited home health care under restrictive, short-term conditions, but not for long-term care. It was designed primarily to help with short-term rehabilitation, usually limited to 100 days, and to get it the following conditions must be met:

- You must have been in a hospital for at least 3 days immediately prior to entering the nursing facility. This eliminates most Alzheimer and Parkinson cases.
- You must go into the facility for the same condition for which you were previously hospitalized, and it must be within 30 days of discharge.
- You must be getting better each day. Once you level off, Medicare stops paying.
- In any case, Medicare covers only skilled nursing care and does not cover intermediate or custodial care at all.

The Solution

Like any other insurance policy you may own, research long-term care policies carefully to find the right policy for your budget and your desired protection. Here are several suggestions to keeping premiums down.

- Buy group coverage. It will be cheaper than individual coverage.
- Employers now offer long-term care insurance as an optional employee benefit. The employee, spouse and employee's parents may be eligible to buy coverage.
- Save money by choosing a longer waiting period, lower benefits or coverage that ends after a certain time frame. However, as with life insurance, the amount of the premiums is not the most important consideration when purchasing long-term care insurance.

Ask the right questions. When shopping for long-term care insurance, compare the following:

- What are premium costs for each plan?
- What is the company's history on payouts and premium increases?
- What are the settings for covered care? Nursing home? Assisted living facility? Home care? Does it cover skilled, intermediate and custodial nursing home care?
- What are the choices of daily maximum?
- Is the policy indexed for inflation and how is the indexing calculated?
- Under what conditions are premiums waived?
- What benefits are covered, besides basic nursing home costs?

- What are the choices for payout/benefit years?
- What other optional benefits are available? At what cost?
- What are the choices for how many days must you wait before coverage starts (referred to as an elimination period or deductible)? Does it only have to be met once?
- Is policy qualified under the Health Insurance and Portability Act of 1996?
- Is the policy guaranteed for life, or can the insurance company cancel it?
- What are the conditions that trigger benefit payments? Do I have to be hospitalized before benefits begin?
- Is there a pre-existing conditions clause?
- Are there specific, guaranteed protections against policy lapses and reinstatements?
- How are benefits paid?
- How long has the company been selling long-term care insurance?
- What are the insurer's financial-strength ratings from the major insurance ratings services (A.M. Best, Standard & Poor's, Moody's and Duff & Phelps)?
- Request a sample copy of the exact contract of the policy you would be purchasing from the company.

Other thoughts:

- Long term care insurance coverage is bought in dollars-per-day payout amounts, usually in $10 increments. Select a cost that will help you offset the daily cost but not necessarily cover the full daily cost.
- The average stay in a skilled nursing facility is 2.8 years. Policies typically cover: 3 or 5 years of care, or unlimited lifetime care. Lifetime costs you more, and 3 years costs the least. Consider purchasing the unlimited lifetime option so payments will not stop midway through your stay.
- Investing in a survivorship rider will free your spouse from further payments upon your death.

As health care costs continue to climb, protecting your investment assets is more important than ever. You owe it to yourself and your family to at least investigate long-term care insurance.

The Resources

www.opm.gov/insure/ltc/

Information on the Federal Long Term Care Insurance Program (FLTCIP).

www.prepsmart.com/update-long-term-care.html

A Website devoted to long term care insurance.

www.life-line.org

Information on how essential role long-term care insurance plays in one's life.

Life Insurance
(Term vs. Permanent)

The Challenge

When you think retirement, do you think stocks, bonds and IRAs? Did you think life insurance? Life insurance is seldom considered an investment tool. The primary reason to purchase life insurance is to provide cash to your family upon your death to replace your income and help your family meet financial obligations like your funeral expenses, medical bills and lawyer's fees. It will also pay your family's daily living expenses, mortgage payments and college tuition so they can continue to live comfortably. That is good short-term strategy, now, think long-term. What would happen if you died prematurely or became disabled before you fully financed your retirement? For the short-term, your family would be fine, for the long-term however, any future retirement planning would die with you.

The Facts

There are two types of life insurance: term and permanent.

Term Insurance
- Provides protection for a specific period of time (or term) and pays a benefit only if you die during the contract term.
- Provides higher levels of coverage at a lower cost than permanent insurance, but does not build any equity or accumulate cash value.
- At the end of the term you can renew the policy, but usually at a higher rate. The younger you are, the cheaper the monthly payments will be.
- To renew the policy, you also may have to show evidence of insurability by taking another medical exam and answering questions about your lifestyle, health status and family history.

Permanent Insurance
- Provides lifelong protection. As long as you pay the premiums and do not take out a loan against the policy, withdraw cash or surrender the policy, the full-face amount will be paid to your beneficiaries when you die. Unlike term insurance, permanent life insurance accumulates cash value.

- Policy premiums remain constant and will not change.
- Builds a fixed or variable cash value or cash-surrender value. Cash values accumulate on a tax-deferred basis just like assets in most retirement and tuition savings plans and can be used in the future for any purpose you wish.
- You can borrow cash value for a down payment on a home, to help pay for your children's education or to provide income for your retirement.
- You can use the cash value to continue your current insurance protection to continue coverage.

With all types of permanent policies, the cash value of a policy is different from the policy's face amount. Face amount is the money that will be paid at death or policy maturity. Cash value is the amount available if you surrender a policy before its maturity or your death. There are different classifications of permanent insurance. The most common include whole life, variable life, universal life and variable universal life.

Whole Life or Ordinary Life

- The most common type of permanent insurance.
- The annual premium is guaranteed to never increase during the life of the policy.
- Earn dividends that can be reinvested to purchase additional insurance or can be applied to defray the premium amount.

Variable Life

- Death benefits and cash values may vary with the performance of the investments included in the portfolio.
- Allocate your premiums among a variety of investment options offering varying degrees of risk: stocks and bonds or a fixed account that guarantees interest and principal.
- A good option for people who do not mind higher risk in return for higher rewards.

Universal Life

- You can pay premiums at any time, in any amount (based on certain minimum and maximums). This type of policy allows you to increase or decrease the death benefit at any time.
- The cash value is not guaranteed because the cash value is linked to the performance of the options you choose to invest in and will fluctuate with market conditions.
- You are guaranteed a minimum amount of death benefits, as long as premiums are sufficient to sustain that death benefit.
- Provide a guaranteed rate of return on your cash values unless the company's portfolio underperforms or premium payments are insufficient.

Variable Universal Life

- Is similar to universal life and also features flexible premiums.
- You can allocate your premium dollars to a variety of investment options, including a fixed account.
- Provides an income tax-free death benefit, has a cash value that grows tax-deferred and is accessible through policy loans and/or withdrawals.
- Allows for increase or decrease of the policy coverage and premium changes to the life insurance benefit option, or you may select the option that guarantees the death benefit with the guaranteed minimum death benefit rider.
- A good option for people who do not mind higher risk in return for higher rewards.

Which insurance policy is best for you?

The Solution

Buying the right amount and the right kind of life insurance could be one of the most important financial decisions you will make. How much insurance do you need? Which policy is best for your family? Sometimes the answer is about how much your family will need after you are gone and how much you can afford to purchase today.

Determining how much life insurance you need requires a careful review of your current and future financial obligations (i.e., a combination of what would it cost for your surviving family members to meet immediate needs like funeral costs, taxes, food, clothing, utilities, mortgage payments, etc. and future obligations like college and retirement funding) and how much insurance will fit into your immediate budget. The most common way to determine your life insurance needs is by conducting what is called a needs analysis. Financial planners estimate you should have 15 to 26 times your salary in life insurance to meet your family's immediate and future financial needs. Begin by evaluating your family's needs. Estimate what each of your family members would need to meet immediate and future financial obligations.

Immediate needs may include:

Final expenses:	$ 25,000
Mortgage:	$ 100,000
Outstanding debts	$ 0
Education	$ 82,000
Total	$ 207,000

Next, figure out how much future income your family would need to maintain their standard of living based on your current income level. If you, at age 45, you earn

$50,000 and would have worked for another 20 years, total lost income would equal $1 million. Factor in a rate of inflation at approximately 3.5 percent and a tax rate of 7 percent, and your present value of income would equal $743,000 in lost income. Add together immediate and future needs to see how much insurance you need.

$$\begin{array}{r} \$\ 207,000 \\ \underline{\$\ 743,000} \\ \$\ 950,000 \end{array}$$

The recommended amount of insurance is $950,000 to meet immediate and future financial obligations and enable your spouse to continue funding a retirement plan. You can secure this benefit amount by purchasing a combination of term and permanent life insurance.

When comparing policies:

- Ask about provisions such as accelerated death benefits, disability waiver of premium and accidental death benefits.
- Price is not the only factor to consider. Some term policies offer an option called a return-of-premium term policy. If you keep the policy in force for the full-term, the insurance company will refund the premium payments you made over that 20-year period. The premiums for return-of-premium policies can be 30 percent to 40 percent higher than premiums for standard term policies.
- Look for term policies that offer convertibility. This gives you the option of converting your term policy into a permanent policy, such as whole life, without submitting evidence of insurability.
- Investigate the company's ratings. Several private companies conduct financial analyses of insurance companies and their reports can be found in your local library or can be ordered by phone, mail or online.

While you should not put off an important decision that would provide protection for your family, take the time to make sure you fully understand any policy you are considering. You should be comfortable with the company, agent and product before purchasing anything.

The Resources

visit *www.life-line.org*

> For information about life insurance and the essential role it plays in sound financial planning.

Estate
Planning

The Challenge

Successful estate planning transfers your assets to your beneficiaries quickly and usually with minimal tax consequences. Your estate is everything you own, either individually or jointly, and includes real property (land and buildings) and personal property (jewelry, cars, collections, furniture, investments, etc.)

You should have an estate plan if you:

- Are the parent of minor children.
- Own property that you care about.
- Care about your health care treatment.
- Have family member you care about.

If you do not have minor children or others who you want to pass your assets to, do not care about your property and have no concerns about your health care treatment, then you do not need an estate plan. But if any one of these categories is important to you, then you should have an estate plan.

The process of estate planning includes inventorying your assets and making a will and/or establishing a trust, often with an emphasis on minimizing taxes. Determining how you should distribute your assets depends on the amount of your estate. Consult an attorney, CPA or tax advisor to determine if a simple will is sufficient to protect your estate or if you need to establish a more complex family or living trust or foundation for added protection.

The only time that you can prepare and implement an estate plan is while you are alive and have legal capacity to enter into a contract. There is no time like the present to get started.

The Facts

Several documents are typically included as part of the estate planning process.

A Will/Last Will and Testament

Transfers property you hold in your name to the beneficiaries—the people and organizations you specify in your will to have it. A will also names someone you select to be your executor, or the person who carries out the terms of the will, and a guardian, or the person you name to care for your minor children.

A Durable Power of Attorney for Health Care/Health Care Proxy

Appoints a person of your choice to make decisions regarding your health care treatment in the event that you are unconscious or unable to make decisions.

A Living Will/Directive to Physicians

Is an advance directive that gives doctors and hospitals your instructions regarding the extent of your care in the event you suffer permanent incapacity, such as an irreversible coma.

A Durable Power of Attorney for Property

Appoints a person of your choice to act for you and handle financial matters should you be unable or perhaps unavailable to do so.

A Living Trust

Can be used to hold legal title to and provide a mechanism to manage your property. You can select the person or persons you want, even yourself, as the trustee(s) to carry out the trust instructions and name one or more successor trustees to take over if you cannot. A trust is effective immediately and continues in force for the duration of your lifetime and after your death.

A Family Limited Partnership

Is typically used for large estates with a need for specialized estate planning in order to minimize federal and state estate/death/inheritance taxes and to protect assets.

Regardless of the size of your estate, estate planning will benefit your heirs. If your estate is worth less than $2 million, your estate planning may be easy to implement. However, if your estate is worth more than $2 million, you should review your estate plan carefully to minimize the amount of taxes your beneficiaries will pay upon your death. That is because taxable estates worth in excess of current limits are taxed at rates as high as 45 percent to 50 percent.

There are a number of ways you can reduce the amount of taxes your estate will pay upon your death:

- Donate your assets during your lifetime to a 501(3)c charitable organization.
- Give each beneficiary an annual gift of $12,000. These gifts are tax-free but also have some restrictions attached. Federal tax law permits you to transfer assets to your spouse without incurring gift or estate taxes, regardless of the amount.

Bypass trusts or credit shelter trusts can give a couple the advantages of the marital deduction while utilizing the unified credit to its fullest. With a bypass or credit shelter trust, the first spouse to die can leave the amount shielded by the applicable credit to the trust. The trust can provide income to the surviving spouse for life, then upon the death of the surviving spouse the assets are distributed to beneficiaries, such as children.

The Solution

The best time to start an estate plan is now, while you have full mental capacity. Procrastination is the number one reason why estate plans are never completed. Putting off your estate planning obviously will not affect you, but it will have a big impact on your beneficiaries upon your death. Even if your estate is not likely to be subject to federal estate taxes, estate planning is necessary to be sure your intentions and distribution of your assets are carried out.

The first step in estate planning is to inventory everything you own and assign a value to each asset. Here is a list to help get you started. You may need to delete some categories or add others.

- residence and other real estate
- savings (bank accounts, CDs, money markets)
- investments (stocks, bonds, mutual funds)
- 401(k), IRA, pension and other retirement accounts
- life insurance policies and annuities
- ownership interest in a business
- motor vehicles (cars, boats, planes)
- jewelry
- collectibles
- other personal property

Next follow these simple steps to successful estate planning:

- Add the value of your home, investments, retirement savings and life insurance policies to determine your total estate value.
- Determine if you are best served by a will, a living trust or both.
- Consider minimizing probate costs through gifting strategies, living trusts, and insurance or annuity contracts, as appropriate.
- Explore the possibility of qualifying for survivorship (also known as second to die) life insurance held outside of the estate to pay for estate taxes.
- Review all property and asset purchases. Make sure the deed, car title and bank accounts are set up as joint tenancies with the right of survivorship. This means that both owners have equal access to the property. In the event that one tenant should die, the co-owner acquires 100 percent ownership without incurring tax liability.
- Outline your estate plan in writing and review it regularly with a trusted

professional as tax laws are adjusted or changed.

- Consult with qualified legal and tax advisers to maintain a well-crafted estate plan. A certified financial planner and/or an insurance agent experienced in estate planning and settlement can also be very helpful.
- Responsible adult children can help reduce ongoing legal costs if one or more of them are able to serve as trustee of any trusts held outside the taxable estate.
- Several software programs and interactive Websites are available to help you organize your estate planning ideas.
- Read all legal agreements carefully and seek a second opinion if you have any doubts about sections in the documents.
- Never sign anything you do not understand or with which you do not agree.
- Do not forget to include special instructions and trusts for grandchildren if you wish to make separate accommodations for them in your plan.

Keep in mind that estate planning is not a one-time job. There are a number of changes that may call for a review of your plan. Take a fresh look at your estate plan if:

- The value of your assets changes significantly;
- You marry, divorce or remarry;
- You have a child;
- You move to a different state;
- The executor of your will or the administrator of your trust dies or becomes incapacitated, or your relationship with that person changes significantly;
- One of your heirs dies or has a permanent change in health; or
- The laws affecting your estate change.

The Resources

www.aarp.org

AARP provides additional information about estate planning.

www.irs.gov

http://law.freeadvice.com/estate_planning/

Freeadvice.com provides legal information and resources on estate planning.

Put It
Into a Trust

The Challenge

A trust is a good way to protect your assets both during your life and after you are gone. There are several advantages to setting up a trust:

- A trust can provide financial security for your children and your spouse.
- Trusts are not public documents; your affairs remain private.
- Trusts can provide financially for your spouse, children or others that you want to care for after your death.
- Trusts may minimize your tax exposure. If you set up the right kind of trust for your estate, you can reduce the amount of tax burden in the present and future. The creation of a trust allows you a certain amount of control of how the assets held by the trust are handled. For example, if you wish to leave money to someone who may not be mature enough to handle money, you can specify that the money can only be used for health, education, support and maintenance of that person until the age of 35. After age 35 the remaining income and principal will be distributed.
- Your estate will most likely avoid probate.
- You control how the money can be allocated, when and how long.
- Special needs trusts will ensure that your beneficiaries who are developmentally disabled or mentally ill can receive inheritances without losing access to essential government benefits.

No single trust can accomplish everything you want to achieve. To reduce your taxes, for example, you have to put your property into a permanent and unchangeable (irrevocable) trust, but trusts you establish solely to manage your assets can be changed (revocable) as your circumstances change.

Creating a trust can be expensive and most financial planners agree that unless your estate is worth in excess of $2 million, it may not be worth the expense. However, there are other reasons why you may need to create a trust: beneficiaries may be too young to manage a large sum of money, a disabled child may need continuous care through a guardianship or a spouse or other family members may seize control of the money unless you put restrictions in place. The point being is that whether you want to avoid probate and taxes or provide for heirs that may need protection, a trust may be the best way to go for your estate. How would a trust benefit your beneficiaries?

The Facts

To expedite the transferring of assets to beneficiaries, some individuals choose to arrange their property so that it can bypass the probate process upon their deaths. For example, placing property into a trust before death (as opposed to a straight will) will often avoid probate. Similarly, jointly held property, such as life insurance, annuities, 401(k)s or IRAs will also avoid probate and allow property to transfer to beneficiaries outside the probate process.

You can also establish a by-pass trust in which the trust holds property for your children and provides for your surviving spouse during his or her lifetime.

There are different types of trusts, designed for different types of planning, and formed in different ways:

A Testamentary Trust

Is created by your will, funded by your estate and administered by a trustee named in your will. Obviously this trust is created after your death. Its primary goal is saving estate taxes and appointing someone to manage the assets in the trust.

A Living or Inter Vivos Trust

Is set up while you are alive. You serve as the trustee and name a successor to take over when you die or are unable to serve. Its primary goal is to manage your estate assets and oversee the transfer of property outside probate.

A Pour-Over Trust

Is also created while you are alive but is funded when you die. Its primary purpose is to receive one-time payouts like life insurance or pension benefits or the any portion of your estate that is left over.

There are two types of trusts: revocable and irrevocable.

- A revocable trust can be modified. You can change beneficiaries, replace the trustee or end the trust completely.
- An irrevocable trust cannot be modified or changed in any way.

Trusts can be created based on the size of the estate and the wishes of the benefactor.

- A living trust can be used to hold legal title to and provide a mechanism to manage your property. You can select the person or persons you want, even yourself, as the trustee(s) to carry out the trust instructions and name one or more successor trustees to take over if you cannot. A living trust is effective immediately and continues in force for the duration of your lifetime and continues after your death.

- A family limited partnership trust is typically used for large estates with a need for specialized estate planning in order to minimize federal and state estate/death/inheritance taxes and to protect assets.
- Bypass trusts or credit shelter trusts can give a couple the advantages of the marital deduction while utilizing the unified credit to its fullest. With a bypass or credit shelter trust, the first spouse to die can leave the amount shielded by the applicable credit to the trust. The trust can provide income to the surviving spouse for life, and upon the death of the surviving spouse the assets are distributed to beneficiaries, such as children.
- A life insurance trust is a common trust, usually irrevocable, that is permitted by its terms to buy insurance. The trust should be authorized to hold a wide range of investment vehicles, with no requirement that life insurance be purchased. Proceeds from policies you own will be included in your estate, even though paid to a third party.

The Solution

A trust is an excellent vehicle to protect your assets during your life and after you pass away. It can provide financial security for your children and your spouse. The following tips will help you successfully set up a trust.

- A living trust is one in which assets are used and controlled by you during your lifetime and are distributed when you die as directed by the trust. The probate process is avoided for assets put into the trust.
- A testamentary trust, like a living trust, also takes effect when you die. It is usually tied to a will and can help eliminate or reduce estate taxes for your beneficiaries. Unlike a living trust, a testamentary trust does not avoid probate.
- Set up the trust once you have determined the type you need and choose who you want as your trustee (the person responsible for ensuring that the terms of the trust agreement are carried out).
- Trusts do not necessarily exempt your estate from estate taxes. Consult with your bank, attorney or certified financial adviser to understand the full benefits of a trust.
- Obtain the appropriate documents from your adviser (or purchase a software program to assist you) and complete them to set up the trust.
- When deciding how to fund a living trust, identify which assets to include. These are the assets over which you have control and wish to control during your lifetime.

- Name a successor trustee who will administer the assets in your living trust in the event you become incapacitated for any reason. A trustee should be financial savvy and be able to make decisions impartially. It is sometimes wise to use an attorney, financial planner or another professional as your trustee. Not only must trustees exercise impartiality, they must be available as long as the trust exists. Choose wisely and designate successor trustees as well.
- Keep in mind that even if an asset is mentioned in your living trust documents, it is not considered trust property unless ownership has been transferred to the trust.
- Some assets do not need to be placed into trust. Retirement savings, bank accounts for which you have signed payable on death declarations and life insurance proceeds go directly to beneficiaries named with the respective institutions, generally tax-free.

Every situation is unique. Although your total estate value may not meet the recommended guidelines of $2 million to set up a trust, there may be other circumstances or goals you wish to achieve through a trust. Talk with your tax advisor or banker to discuss your options.

The Resources

For further information on trusts, visit:

www.trusts&estates.com

The Journal of Wealth Management for Estate-Planning Professionals.

www.law.cornell.edu/wex/index.php/Estates_and_Trusts

Overview of estates and trusts.

www.wsba.org/media/publications/pamphlets/trusts.htm

Comprehensive trust pamphlet from the Washington State Bar Association.

The Power
of a Will

The Challenge

Most individuals are aware that they need a will, yet nearly 75 percent do not have one. Of the 25 percent who do, approximately half of these wills are out of date or invalid for one reason or another. The only way to ensure that your property, investments and personal effects will be distributed after your death according to your wishes is to prepare a will.

A will is a legal document that transfers your property, after you die. It names the people who will care for your children if they are minors, and the people who will execute the terms of your will. If typed, most states require that the will be signed in the presence of two witnesses. Some states allow *holographic* wills, which means that significant portions must be entirely written in the handwriting of the testator–with no witnesses required. A little know fact is that many states consider holographic wills invalid. A deathbed or oral will is known as a *nuncupative* will.

Taking the time to prepare your will now can save your heirs significant expense and trouble later. If you have young children, having a will is extremely important because it enables you to designate a guardian for them in the event of your death. If you do not already have a will, now is the time to write one. If you already have a will and have had a change in circumstances, it is time to update it.

The Facts

Many people mistakenly believe that if a married person dies without a will (intestate) then the surviving spouse automatically retains all the deceased spouse's property, especially if there are young children. This is not necessarily true; most states may award one-third to one-half of the decedent's property to the surviving spouse and the remainder to the children, regardless of their age. If there are no children, most states give only one-third to one-half of the estate to the survivor. The remainder may go to the decedent's parents, if alive. If both parents are dead, many states split the remainder among the decedent's siblings.

If you die without a will or relatives, your estate *escheats*, or is turned over to the state to administer. If there are no apparent heirs, the state may claim your entire estate.

Whether you have a valid will or not when you die, your estate will most likely go through *probate*. Probate is the legal process to ensure the decedent's property is rightfully transferred to his or her heirs and/or beneficiaries. If there is no property to transfer, there is usually no need for probate. The probate court determines if the will is valid, hears any objections to the will, orders that creditors be paid and supervises the process to ensure that property remaining is distributed in accordance with the terms and conditions of the will. Another function of probate is to provide for the collection of any taxes due by reason of the deceased's death or on the transfer of his or her property. Taxes are generally paid 9 months after death and must be paid in cash before assets can be passed on to beneficiaries.

An estate becomes a taxable entity upon the death of an individual and continues to exist until all the assets are disbursed to the heirs. The personal representative or executor will file tax returns for the estate, IRS *Form 706* to show estate assets and an estate income tax return, IRS *Form 1041* to report any income generated by the estate. It is wise to consult a tax attorney, financial planner or accountant regarding the best distribution of your estate to help your heirs avoid excessive taxes and penalties.

The Solution

Preparing a will is simple. There are a number of software products and pre-printed forms available today. Start by outlining your objectives, inventorying your assets, estimating your outstanding debts and preparing a list of family members and friends who will be beneficiaries.

All your assets should be mentioned in your will. Any items not specifically mentioned may be addressed in a catchall clause of your will called a *residuary* clause. The residuary clause generally begins "I give the remainder of my estate to . . ." Without this clause, items not specifically mentioned will be treated differently and distributed in accordance with state law.

Your will should include:

- Your name and place of residence.
- A brief description of your assets.
- Names of spouse, children and other beneficiaries, such as charities or friends.
- Alternate beneficiaries, in the event a beneficiary dies before you;

- Specific gifts or bequeaths, such as an automobile or residence.
- Establishment of trusts, if desired.
- Cancellation of debts owed to you, if desired.
- Name of an executor to manage the estate.
- Name of a guardian for minor children and an alternative in the event your first choice is unable or unwilling to act.
- Your signature.
- Witnesses' signatures.

Be specific and clear when naming beneficiaries. For example, state the person's full name as well as his or her relationship to you (child, cousin, friend, etc.) so your executor will know exactly whom you mean. Clarity will also help to prevent future legal challenges to your will and hard feelings among family members.

When composing your will there are several things you can do in your will and other things you cannot do, unless you welcome a legal challenge.

- You can limit the amount of inheritance to one or more of your children, or leave them nothing at all. Some states do not allow you to disinherit your children. If you decide to leave nothing to your son Timmy, make sure you state that directly in the will or you may leave Timmy a small token, like your pet rock collection.
- You can specify if the heirs of your beneficiaries inherit their share if they die before you do. For example, if Timmy dies before you do, you may designate that his children inherit his portion your pet rock collection.
- You can include a clause that provides that anyone who contests the will loses any share they might have received. This clause is called in *terrorem* and may only be used in certain states.
- You cannot disinherit a spouse as long as you are legally married.
- You cannot impose conditions on heirs that are illegal or reckless. Thus, you cannot tie an heir's right to an inheritance based on winning the million-dollar lottery or divorcing a spouse.
- You cannot write in changes and cross items out of the will after it has been signed and witnessed. Changes must be made through a legally executed codicil or amendment or through the writing of a new will to nullify the old will.

States require that you sign the will in front of witnesses. Although the number of witnesses varies by state, generally two is sufficient. A witness should not be a beneficiary of your will. Only one copy should be signed.

Two of the most important items included in your will are (1) naming a guardian for minor children and (2) naming an executor. Without a will, the court will step in and choose the person responsible for wrapping up your affairs.

It should be noted that a living will is not a part of your will. It is a separate document that lets your family members know what type of care you do or do not want to receive should you become terminally ill or permanently unconscious. It becomes effective only when you cannot express your wishes yourself. If your state recognizes a power of attorney for health care, have one executed to authorize someone to act in accordance with your present intentions. Discuss with family members your wishes outlined in your living will and be sure they have a signed copy.

Once your will is written, store it in a safe place that is accessible to others after your death. If you name a trust company as executor, it will hold your will in safekeeping. You can keep it in your safe deposit box, but be aware that some states will seal your safe deposit box upon your death, so this may not always be the safest place to store your will. Make sure a close friend or relative knows where to find your will. If you had an attorney prepare your will, have him or her retain a copy with a note stating where the original can be found.

Periodically review and update your will as your circumstances change. You can update your will by amending it by way of a codicil or by drawing up a new one. Generally, people choose to issue a new will that supersedes the old document. Be sure to sign the new will and have it witnessed, and then destroy the old one.

The Resources

www.doyourownwill.com/glossary.asp

For definitions of terms frequently used in wills.

http://law.freeadvice.com/tax_law/estate_tax_law

Freeadvice.com provides advice on estate planning.

Naming an
Executor

The Challenge

As mentioned in the previous chapter, most individuals are aware that they need a will, yet most do not have one. Of the 25 percent who do have a will, it is estimated that one-half of the wills are out of date. Everyone procrastinates for different reasons, but writing a will does not have to be complicated or expensive. The only way to ensure that your property, investments and personal effects will be distributed after your death according to your wishes it to prepare a will.

One component of creating a will is to name an executor or personal representative to carry out your wishes and to make sure the estate is properly administered upon your death. An executor (male) or executrix (female) is the person you are putting in charge to settle your estate in accordance with your wishes or to carry out the terms of your will.

Your executor should be a trustworthy person with common sense and good judgment, who will treat everyone fairly. You might choose a trusted friend or relative who is capable of handling financial matters. Determining who is the best man or woman for the job is the challenge.

The Facts

The job of executor is a serious task and should be assigned to someone who is detail oriented and can manage a lot of paperwork.

A list of duties the executor will oversee includes:

- Gathering information of beneficiary names and locating copies of the will and other important papers. If the executor is named in advance, this information can be provided to the person while you are alive to make the job easier.

- Determining whether probate proceedings are required. Probate laws vary by state and depend on the value of the estate. If probate is necessary, then the executor files the appropriate legal documents with the local probate court. If probate is required, the executor must apply to appear before the probate court.
- Managing the affairs of the estate, such as paying bills and taxes, canceling subscriptions and making decision as needed. Probate can take a full year to complete.
- Filing a final income tax return for the estate, covering the period from the beginning of the last year of your life until the date of death. Depending on the value of your assets, estate taxes may be owed. Usually this tax return is filed about 9 months after the date of death.
- Sending notices to all creditors and vendors notifying them of your death, including health care providers, banks, government agencies, such as Social Security and Veterans Administration, brokerage companies, credit card companies and any other creditors.
- Providing certified copies of your death certificate (several will be needed) to vendors and creditors to close accounts, coordinate stock transfers, terminate leases and arrange for the sale of property. Proof of your death will be required for these transactions and for filing insurance claims.
- Ensuring that beneficiaries receive the assets left to them as specified in your will.

If your estate is particularly large and complex, you may wish to appoint an executor team consisting of a relative or friend and an estate lawyer or an accountant. This provides your estate with the benefit of someone who knew you well and has a sense of how you might have liked issues handled and a professional who can guide your estate through the maze of tax laws. With a team, one executor may handle the bulk of the work and hand off the financial or legal issues to the professional for a pre-arranged fee.

The Solution

You can choose whomever you want to be your executor, be it a spouse, adult child, attorney or other financial professional. However, since the person will be dealing with the emotional mixture of family, grief and money, it is best to choose someone who you feel has the sensitivity and strength to stick to your financial wishes. Your first instinct might be to name a lawyer, financial planner or tax attorney, but the person you choose only needs to have enough common sense to take over the administrator duties, and often friends or family may be the most familiar with you wishes.

Many banks offer executor services, but they also charge for the service. In most cases, when a friend or relative agrees to become your executor, he or she will most likely waive the fee, although it is common for the executor to accept a fee equivalent to 1 percent to 3 percent of the total estate. Check with your state laws as this amount is state regulated. When you make a will, it is very important to include in the will specifics on how much the executor should be paid.

If an executor is not named in a will, a probate judge will appoint one to oversee your estate. Sometimes family conflict can develop over who should be appointed by the judge. If this happens, a neutral lawyer may be appointed and must be paid with estate funds. Be aware that the administrator may have to pay certain fees or post a bond at the expense of your estate before he or she can begin to distribute your assets.

There are restrictions as to who may serve as an executor.

- States will recognize executors who are residents of the same state. If you want to select a non-resident executor, make sure to also appoint a co-executor who resides in the state.
- Name a second choice or back up executor in case your first choice refuses or is unable to serve.
- An executor must be a competent adult, a U.S. citizen and cannot be a convicted felon.
- Several states require that the executor post a bond to protect the assets of the estate. There are usually waivers available in most states that would excuse the executor from posting a bond. You can specify in your will that your executor and the guardian of your minor children serve without bond. If you die intestate (without a will) you will not have this option; the judge will assign a guardian or executor who must be bonded and the bonding fee will be taken out of your estate.

If you name an executor who you would also like to leave money to, their executor fee will be paid before estate taxes are taken out, essentially allowing you to bequeath money to them before the government takes its cut. Check with your tax advisor. There are ways to structure payouts to minimize the tax liability on beneficiaries. For example, if you have an estate value of $650,000, you can request to have your daughter paid an executor fee of $50,000, bringing the value of your estate below $600,000. Your estate will pay lower taxes on the value and your daughter will pay a lower tax rate on the $50,000 fee.

The Resources

www.gottrouble.com/legal/estate_planning/funerals_executors_role.html.

Additional information regarding wills and executors.

www.irs.gov

For IRS *Publication 559*, which contains valuable information and instructions for survivors, executors and administrators of estates.

www.doyourownwill.com

This Website provides a simple and inexpensive way to compose your own legal will online.

Probate

The Challenge

The word probate comes from Latin and means *to prove*, in this case to prove in court the existence of a will and to authenticate the will. Probate is the process that transfers legal title of property from the estate of the person who has died to his or her heirs. If there is no property to transfer, there is usually no need for probate. Another function of probate is to provide the state in which the decedent lived a way of collecting death benefit taxes from the estate before assets are disbursed.

Probate can be a slow and expensive process, especially if the will is contested. Even for an uncontested will, the cost to move an estate through the probate process can add up to as much as 3 percent to 7 percent of the total estate value.

In this chapter we will discuss ways to keep your estate out of probate, reduce your tax liability and transfer your assets to your heirs faster.

The Facts

One of the biggest problems with probate is that it can cause a delay of distribution of your assets for 6 months or longer after your death. This delay provides the executor enough time to make an accounting of all your property and assets and to publish a notice of your death in the local newspaper. Creditors are also notified and have a specific time period in which to make claims against your estate. The executor settles these debts out of assets and distributes the remainder of the assets to your heirs in accordance with your will.

If your estate had more debts than assets, the probate court will make the determination on how to distribute your assets to creditors. If creditors are unable to make a valid claim prior to the close of probate, they are out of luck and cannot require your heirs to pay the debt. That is however, unless you co-signed a loan for a parent, for example, you cannot be held accountable for your parents' debts upon their death.

Occasionally lenders will try going after the children of deceased creditors to get them to pay an unpaid bill, even after the close of the estate's probate. Heirs have no legal obligation to pay debts that the estate cannot otherwise pay. Be aware that these attempts are strictly illegal.

Not all of your property must go through probate. Many states allow certain types of property to pass to named beneficiaries free of probate, or through a simplified probate procedure. Real and personal property owned as a joint tenancy passes to the surviving co-owner(s) without going through probate. Most named beneficiary policies, such as life insurance, annuities, IRAs, Keoghs and 401(k) accounts, transfer automatically outside of probate. Bank accounts that are set up as payable-on-death or set up in trust for are also exempt from probate. And if a living trust has been set up to hold legal title to some of your property, the property will pass to your heirs without probate. If you own property outside of the state you reside in, the property will be submitted to probate in that state. A separate procedure is started called an ancillary probate and may require a local executor to manage that property through probate.

While there is no requirement to use a lawyer, probate is a rather formalistic procedure. One minor omission, such as the failure to send a family member a copy of the petition or a missed deadline, can cause everything to come to a grinding halt or expose everyone to liability.

A will contest occurs when someone files an objection to the will or produces another will. Will contests can be extraordinarily costly and create long delays. The good news is that not just anyone can contest a will. To properly contest a will a person must have standing to object. Generally, spouses, children and heirs have standing to contest a will.

When all the costs are added up—and the costs may include appraisal costs, executor's fees, court costs, costs for a type of insurance policy known as a surety bond, plus legal and accounting fees—probate can easily cost between 3 percent to 7 percent of the total estate value. If there is a will contest, the cost can be substantially more.

The Solution

Clearly, you want your estate distributed as quickly as possible and to avoid the slow and expensive process of probate. There are ways to minimize how much of your estate is included in probate or even avoid it altogether.

- Payable-on-death bank accounts offer an easy way to your keep money, even large sums, out of probate. Your bank can provide a form allowing you to name the person you want to inherit the money in your account at your death. The probate court is never involved.

- When you open a retirement account, such as an IRA or 401(k), you must name a beneficiary. After your death the beneficiary can claim the money directly from the account custodian.
- The Uniform Transfer-on-Death Securities Registration Act lets you name someone to inherit your stocks, bonds or brokerage accounts without probate. Similar to the payable-on-death bank account, you designate a beneficiary when you register your ownership.The beneficiary has no rights to the stock as long as you are alive, but may claim the securities without probate when you die.
- A few states offer car owners the convenient option of naming a beneficiary on their certificate of registration. Simply register the vehicle in beneficiary form. The new registration certificate will list the name of the beneficiary, who will automatically own the vehicle after your death.
- Forms of joint ownership, such as joint tenancy, provide an easy way to avoid probate when the first owner dies.
- Holding title to major assets in a form of joint ownership or joint tenancy with right of survivorship avoids probate. This is a good idea when purchasing real estate, a home, car or boat together. Setting up a joint tenancy is easy, and it does not cost a penny.
- In some states, married couples often take title in tenancy by the entirety. It is very similar to joint tenancy, but can be used only by married couples. Both types of ownership avoid probate.
- Another way to co-own property with your spouse is available to you if you live in a community property state. In those states, you and your spouse may own property as community property with the right of survivorship. When one spouse dies, the other automatically owns the asset. Transferring title to the survivor is simple and does not require court proceedings.
- Holding your valuable property in a revocable living trust avoids probate because the property is owned by the trust. After your death, the trustee can easily and quickly transfer the trust property to the family or friends you specify, without probate.
- Giving away property while you are alive helps you avoid probate because what you do not own when you die does not go through probate. If you give away enough assets as gifts, your estate may be small enough to qualify for a streamlined small estate probate procedure after your death. Be aware, however, that if you give away the bulk of your estate in less than 3 years before your death, the state may think you were trying to avoid paying state taxes on your estate and may challenge the tax-exempt status of the gifts.

Almost every state now offers streamlined probate proceedings for small estates. Each state defines that term differently. There are two basic kinds of probate shortcuts for small estates:

1. Claiming Property With Affidavits–No Court Required
   If the total value of all the assets you leave behind is below a pre-set amount and real estate is not included in your total assets, your estate may be able to skip probate entirely. The beneficiary completes an affidavit stating he or she is entitled to a certain item of property under a will or state law and the bank or executor holding the property will release it to the beneficiary.
2. Simplified Court Procedures
   The probate court is still involved, but it exercises less control over the settling of the estate. This procedure is easy enough to handle without a lawyer, so it saves money as well as time.

As you can see, there are ways to minimize how much of your estate can be subject to probate. Keep in mind that even without challenges or complications, settling an estate can take anywhere from 6 months to 2 years before the executor may be released from his or her duties. Careful planning and updating your will on a regular basis will eliminate problems and challenges from disappointed heirs.

The Resources

www.legal-database.com/probatelaw.htm

For terms and definitions associated with probate.

www.law.cornell.edu/uniform/probate.html

To determine if your state has adopted the Uniform Probate Law.

www.nolo.com/encyclopedia/articles/ep/ep15-4l.html
http://law.freeadvice.com/esttatre_planning/trusts.

Both these Websites offer additional information on probate.

Getting Organized

The Challenge

Planning is the easy part, keeping track of all your investments can be a full-time job. Imagine how an executor may struggle if your assets are invisible or difficult to track. Hours upon hours will be needed to track down creditors, beneficiaries and assets. Settling the estate could take years, and paying an executor over this time can take a big bite out of the money you intended to go to heirs. Estates do not need to be complicated to bring the process to a grinding halt. An estate worth $50,000 in Texas took more than 2 years to finalize because beneficiaries were difficult to track down.

How are your affairs organized? If someone had to step in today to finalize your estate, would it be a smooth process or a bumpy road? A well-organized estate will keep the process on track for a quick resolution.

The Facts

Immediately following the death of a loved one, confusion can reign. The will might be missing or a new one may suddenly appear. If the executor must search for creditors, beneficiaries or assets, closing your estate may come to a grinding halt or be delayed for months. It is up to you to make sure to provide the executor with the tools to make the transfer of your assets smooth and problem-free.

As mentioned in Chapter 47: *Naming an Executor*, the job of executor is a serious task that may take up to a year to complete while overseeing hundreds of details, including:

- Gathering beneficiary names and locating copies of the will and other important papers.
- Determining whether probate proceedings are required. Probate laws vary by state and depend on the value of the estate.
- Managing the affairs of the estate, such as paying bills, taxes, canceling subscriptions and making decision as needed.

- Filing a final income tax return for the estate, covering the period from the beginning of the last year of your life until the date of death.
- Sending notices to all creditors and vendors notifying them of your death, including health care providers, banks, government agencies, such as Social Security and Veterans Administration, brokerage companies, credit card companies and any other creditors.
- Obtaining certified copies of your death certificate to provide to vendors and creditors to close accounts, coordinate stock transfers, terminate leases and arrange for the sale of property.
- Ensuring that beneficiaries receive the assets left to them as specified in the will.

The Solution

To organize your affairs, get a binder to keep all your official documents together in one place. The binder will contain most of the information the executor and your family will need to settle your estate. Divide the binder into the following eight sections:

1. Letter of instruction

This is a letter that includes instructions to your heirs. This document summarizes the contents of the binder and provides any other important information, such as deposit box accounts, life insurance policies and user names and passwords. It may also list the attorney who handled your will and any other important, last minute instructions you would like to share with your heirs. This may include any burial or special ceremony requests, pre-arranged funeral home burial instructions or ceremonial requests such as "I want to be dressed in my black suit and blue suede shoes." If you have any special distribution instructions, such as "Aunt Martha is to receive my complete coin collection and Sandy Smith is to receive my stamp collection," be sure to add these types of requests as part of your will.

2. Checklist

The checklist provides a summary of the entire contents of the binder, similar to a table of contents. This lets the executor know exactly what is included in the binder.

3. The Survivor's Report

The Survivor's Report is specifically written for your spouse or children who may have joint ownership of property or bank accounts with you. This report provides specific password information, safety deposit box information and other data that you think will be helpful for everyday living by survivors.

4. Caretaker's Report

If you have a signed power of attorney or Health Care Power of Attorney, these documents should also be included in the binder. If you are uncomfortable leaving a notarized copy in the binder, then put a copy in the binder and leave the notarized copy in a safe deposit box or with your attorney.

5. Financial Reports

Provide copies of your checking and savings accounts, including bank names and bank contacts. If you have an IRA or get Social Security or pension benefits, also include information about required minimum distributions. If you own property, indicate where copies of the deed may be found. If there is a mortgage or line of credit you are still paying, provide lender names and property tax information (amount due and when). Also, if you have any association dues or monthly assessment fees, provide the amount and when they are due.

6. Home Inventory with Photographs

Maintain a complete inventory of all your possessions by taking pictures or producing a videotape. This is also excellent proof of existence for your insurance company in the event of a flood, fire or burglary. Store the photos in a photo album by room. Label each photo with a short history or story about how it was acquired or, if an heirloom, how it has been passed down through generations. This is also a wonderful way to keep the history alive and provide significance and historic value to items you are passing to your heirs. It is also very helpful for documenting valuable jewelry or collector's items that may be displayed in the home or kept in a relative's home for safekeeping if the owner is living in a nursing home or assisted living facility.

7. Annuity and Special Forms

Include copies of any annuities, stock certificates, life insurance policies, bearer bonds, CDs or money market accounts. If you have pledged any funds to a religious or charitable organization, make sure to include where and when the pledge is due.

8. Contact Information

Provide a list of contacts, including names, address, phone numbers and email addresses. Include anyone who manages or handles any of your investments, real estate or legal affairs. Separate the list into categories such as friends, neighbors, investments, etc.

Make your list as complete as possible, including heirs and friends you would like notified of your passing. Your list may include:

- Executor(s)
- Beneficiaries
- Lawyer(s)
- Investment advisor(s), stock broker(s), money fund manager(s), life insurance agent(s) or CPA(s)
- Credit card and finance companies
- Family members
- Friends
- Neighbors and business acquaintances

Finally:

- Keep everything in a safe deposit box.
- Give the executor of your estate copies of everything and meet once or twice a year to give him or her an update.
- File copies with your lawyer.
- Let family members know who you have named as executor and that your estate will be handled by that person.
- Review and update any documents regularly–at least twice a year. Add or delete any possessions or securities you may have purchased or sold, update addresses and make any other changes dictated by new circumstances.

Just as you may have difficulty keeping track of all your investments, imagine how difficult it would be for your family to locate and manage your assets in the event you became ill or incapacitated. You have worked hard to provide for your family, so make sure they can collect everything they are entitled to receive. Organizing all your information into one handy location is an excellent organizational tool regardless of your age.

The Resources

*www.encouragementpress.com/*letter of instruction

View sample letter of instruction.

Resources for an Enjoyable Retirement

Here is a partial list of Retirement resources to help you jumpstart retirement planning.

General Retirement Websites

https://www.tomorrowsmoney.org/section.cfm/389/466
www.morningstar.com
http://beginnersinvest .about.com/cs/investinglessons/l/blreturnonasset.htm
http://money.cnn.com/
http://online.wsj.com/public/us
http://money.howstuffworks.com/question724.htm How stuff works
http://biz.yahoo.com/edu/ed_retire.html
www.fool.com
www.finance-encyclopedia.com/term/apr
www.investopedia.com
www.womens-finance.com/challenge/payyourself.shtml
www.nwlc.org/display.cfm?section=social%20security
www.activeretirement.com

Calculators

www.bloomberg.com/analysis/calculators/retire.html
www.financeCalc.com
www.lfg.com/LincolnPageServer?LFGPage=/lfg/ipc/index.html
www.principal.com/calculators/retire.htm
www.fundadvice.com/tools/calculators
*http://apps.nasd.com/investor_Information/Tools/Calculators/
    retirement_calc.asp*
www.pine-grove.com/financial%20calculators/roi.htm
www.credit-to-cash-advisor.com/document_120.html
www.dinkytown.net/java/InvestmentReturn.html
www.webcalc.net/calc/business/1052.php
www.mostchoice.com/global/calculators/taxdefer0.cfm
www.efunda.com/formulae/finance/apr_calculator.cfm

Credit Cards

http://cgi.money.cnn.com/tools/debtplanner/debtplanner.jsp
www.creditcards.com
www.bankrate.com
www.federalreserve.gov/pubs/shop/survey.htm

Non-profit Organizations/Memberships

www.aarp.org
www.asec.org
www.nefe.org
www.betterinvesting.org/ Investment education.

Government Resources

www.dol.gov/dol/topic/retirement/index.htm
www.defenselink.mil/militarypay/retirement/calc/index.html
www.bls.gov
www.dol.gov/dol/topic/retirement/index.htm
www.irs.org
www.sec.gov
www.ssa.gov
www.cdc.gov/nchs/howto/w2w/w2welcom.htm

Inflation Data

http://stats.bls.gov/
www.inflationdata.com

Your Retirement Savings

www.investorhome.com/process.htm
www.tiaa-cref.com
www3.troweprice.com/ric/RIC
www.savecalc.com/?gclid=CJ6Aw8eoyYQCFSUySAodKEKHKg
http://fireseeker.com/

Early Retirement

www.how-to-retire.com
http://info.ag.uidaho.edu/Resources/PDFs/CIS1013.pdf

Mutual Funds

http://apps.nasd.com/investor_Information/ea/nasd/mfetf.aspx
http://apps.nasd.com/investor_Information/ea/nasd/mfetf.aspx
www.mfea.com/default.asp
www.ici.org/index.html

Annuities

www.annuity.com
www.annuityadvantage.com
www.annuityadvantage.com/equityindexed.htm
http://powerinvestor.com/Primer/Insurance-and-Annuities/Annuities-Variable-and-Fixed.htm

Securities

www.nasd.com
www.naic.org

Money Markets

www.imoneynet.com/
www.sec.gov/answers/mfmmkt.htm
http://beginnersinvest.about.com/cs/banking/a/062501a.htm

Bonds

www.investingbonds.com
www.moneychimp.com
www.ehow.com/how_16557_calculate-bond-yields.html.

Insurance

www.pacificlife.com/Channel/Educational+Information/Calculators/Power+of+Tax+Deferral.htm
www.opm.gov/insure/ltc/
www.prepsmart.com/update-long-term-care.html
www.life-line.org

Small Business Plans

www.irs.gov/pub/irs-pdf/p560.pdf
www.investopedia.com/university/retirementplans/sepira/
http://personal.fidelity.com/products/retirement/getstart/newacc/sepiracalc.shtml.cvsr

Stocks

www.dogsofthedow.com

Virtual Banks

www.bankofinternet.com/
www.oneunited.com/
www2.fdic.gov/starsmail
www.fdic.gov/consumers/questions/index.html
www2.fdic.gov/edie
www.fdic.gov/deposit/deposits/insured/index.html

Credit Unions

www.ncua.gov/indexdata.html
www.creditunion.coop
www.nafcu.org
www.cuna.org

Credit Scores

www.annualcredtireport.com
www.creditbureaureportsonline.com
www.experian.com
www.transunion.com
www.equifax.com

Medicare

www.seniorjournal.com
www.kff.org/medicare/7067/index.cfm
www.medicare.gov

Estate Planning, Trust, Wills, Legal

www.law.cornell.edu/wex/index.php/Estates_and_Trusts
www.law.cornell.edu/uniform/probate.html
www.wsba.org/media/publications/pamphlets/trusts.htm
www.gottrouble.com/legal/estate_planning/funerals_executors_role.html
www.trusts&estates.com
www.doyourownwill.com
www.legal-database.com/probatelaw.htm
http://law.freeadvice.com/estate_planning/trusts
http://www.dhss.mo.gov/SeniorServices/index.html
http://www.mo.gov/mo/living.htm

Eldercare Locator

Get referrals for local agencies to obtain information and services in your community on issues including home health care, nursing home care, and long-term care insurance by calling 1.800.677.1116.

Index

Titles from Encouragement Press

Available from bookstores everywhere or directly from Encouragement Press. Bulk discounts are available, for information please call 1.253.303.0033

50 plus one Series			
Title	Price	Qty.	Subtotal
Greatest Cities in the World You Should Visit	$14.95 U.S./$19.95 Can.		
Tips When Remodeling Your Home	$14.95 U.S./$19.95 Can.		
Greatest Sports Heroes of All Times (North American edition)	$14.95 U.S./$19.95 Can.		
Tips to Building A Retirement Nest Egg	$14.95 U.S./$19.95 Can.		
Ways To Improve Your Study Habits	$14.95 U.S./$19.95 Can.		
Tips When Hiring & Firing Employees	$14.95 U.S./$19.95 Can.		
Questions When Buying a Car	$14.95 U.S./$19.95 Can.		
Tips to Preventing Identity Theft	$14.95 U.S./$19.95 Can.		
Great Books You Should Have Read (and probably didn't)	$14.95 U.S./$19.95 Can.		
Questions to Ask Your Doctor	$14.95 U.S./$19.95 Can.		

Subtotal	
IL residents add 8.75% sales tax	
Shipping & Handling*	
Total	

* Shipping & Handling

U.S. Orders:	Canadian Orders:
$3.35 for first book	$7.00 for first book
$2.00 for ea. add'l add book	$5.00 for ea. add'l book

4 Ways to Order

Phone: 1.773.262.6565

Web: *www.encouragementpress.com*

Fax: 1.773.262.9765

**Mail: Encouragement Press LLC
1261 West Glenlake
Chicago, IL 60660**

Please make checks payable to: Encouragement Press, LLC *(Orders must be prepaid. We regret that we are unable to ship orders without payment or purchase order)*

Payment Method (check one)
❏ **Check enclosed** ❏ **Visa** ❏ **MasterCard**

_____
card number

_____
signature

_____
Name as it appears on card

expiration date _____

P.O. #_____

Encouragement Press, LLC
1261 West Glenlake • Chicago, IL 60660 • *sales@encouragementpress.com*